The Essential Poets

*BOOK/CASSETTE PACKAGES AVAILABLE

Robert Browning

BORN 7 MAY 1812
DIED 12 DECEMBER 1889

The Essential
BROWNING

Selected and with an
Introduction by
DOUGLAS DUNN

The Ecco Press
New York

To Peter Porter
and Anthony Thwaite

Introduction and selection copyright © 1990 by Douglas Dunn
Published in 1990 by The Ecco Press
26 West 17th Street, New York, N.Y. 10011
Published simultaneously in Canada by
Penguin Books Canada Ltd., Ontario
Printed in the United States of America
Design by Reg Perry
FIRST EDITION

Library of Congress Cataloging-in-Publication Data
Browning, Robert, 1812–1889.
The Essential Browning
selected and with an introduction by Douglas Dunn.
p. cm.—(Essential poets: 13)
I. Dunn, Douglas. II. Title.
III. Series: Essential poets (New York, N.Y.); v. 13.
PR4222.A2D86 1990   821'.8—dc19   88-27329 CIP

ISBN 0-88001-195-5

Portrait of Robert Browning
by Dante Gabriel Rossetti
Courtesy of The Granger Collection,
New York

Cassette recordings of live readings and interviews with
several of the series editors are available directly from
The Ecco Press in handsome book/cassette packages for $15.95
each. Call or write for details. Published by arrangement
with The Listening Library, Old Greenwich, CT. Jason Shinder,
general series interviewer and executive producer, is the
founder and director of The Writers' Voice, New York City.

Contents

❖

Introduction

❖

ROBERT BROWNING was born on May 7, 1812, in the south London suburb of Camberwell. Protective, comfortable, and middle-class, his parents acquiesced in his poetic vocation with an unusual sympathy. For the most part Browning was educated at home. Hired tutors were employed, but Browning's father possessed an extensive library. It seems likely that it was the freedom to plunder this large stock of historical and speculative reading that formed Browning's formidable intelligence. By the age of fourteen he was devoted to Shelley's poetry and to an example that encouraged him to choose and then continue to assert an independent existence as a poet. An attempt to study Greek in 1828 at the University of London proved disagreeable. Contemporaries were to look askance at what must have appeared parental mollycoddling as Browning continued to enjoy the security of his family and avoid the drudgery that prepares a young man to earn a living. By the age of thirty-four, when he married Elizabeth Barrett, he was still dependent on his father's generosity. This fortunate liberty was reinforced by Elizabeth Barrett's income, and the legacy of their friend and supporter John Kenyon in 1856.

As well as being helpful and benevolent, Browning's parents are interesting in that their backgrounds suggest an eclectic "Britishness." Browning *père* was a clerk in the Bank of England. Earlier in life he had been employed on his family's sugar plantation in the West Indies, for which he lacked the necessary bad principles. Browning's future wife was to express remorse that the Barrett fortunes were derived initially from the slave trade. Sarah Anna Wiedemann, Browning's mother, was a Scotswoman of German origins from Dundee. Her evangelical, nonconformist Christianity squared not at all with Shelleyan atheism. As the years passed, Mrs. Browning's genuine piety was one of the factors that encouraged her son to dismantle his attachment to Shelley.

In his young manhood Browning was something of a restless, uncertain, and unsuccessful prodigy, perhaps even precious, and given to a gently dandified appearance. *Pauline* was finished by January 1833. It appeared the following March, at his father's expense, privately, anonymously, and without éclat. Thirty-five years later he referred to it disparagingly as "a boyish work" and stated that "good draughtsmanship" and "right handling" were far beyond his youthful means. He claimed that *Pauline* failed to sell a single copy; but its 1,031 lines of blank verse portray convincingly a gifted craftsmanship, as well as the intensity of his embrace of Shelley, the "Sun-treader." That was what embarrassed Browning later on, as well as that failure of "right handling," by which he meant autobiography and the personal in his poetry.

Paracelsus (1835) and his play *Strafford* (1837) were behind him when he first visited Italy in 1838 in search of the places and atmosphere of *Sordello* (1840). A long, technically dazzling poem in six books and almost 6,000 lines, its confusions and remoteness promoted charges of obscurity which were to bedevil his career at least until the success of *The Ring and the Book* (1868–1869). Jane Carlyle read it without ever being sure if Sordello was a man, a city, or a book. Another reader's understanding flagged so seriously that he suspected the effort had reduced him to idiocy. Again, the cost of publication was borne by Browning's father. Bibliographers tell us that it took fifteen years to sell 150 copies. On such a tiny readership was Browning's reputation for obscurity carried. Almost thirty years later, his disdain was impenitent, when, in the closing lines of *The Ring and the Book,* he addressed his readers:

> *So, British Public, who may like me yet,*
> *(Marry and amen!) learn one lesson hence*

> *Of many which whatever lives should teach:*
> *This lesson, that our human speech is naught,*
> *Our human testimony false, our fame*
> *And human estimation words and wind.*
> *Why take the artistic way to prove so much?*
> *Because, it is the glory and good of Art,*
> *That Art remains the one way possible*
> *Of speaking truth, to mouths like mine, at least.*

His interest in the theater must have looked more attractive after the bitingly limited welcome granted to *Sordello*. Here too, though, his progress ran up against failure. William Macready, the actor-manager, soon lost patience with the importunate Browning. "Read Browning's play," he noted on August 3, 1840, "and with the deepest concern I yield to the belief that he will *never write again*—to any purpose."

Drama and the dramatic were mainstays of a temperament that was to lead Browning toward the fiction-making sagacity of his best work. To over-Freudianize his flight from self and his subsequent dislike of autobiography and the personal in poetry is to risk a grudging perspective on Browning's poetry and the virtually prurient excitements of a detective work calculated to spot leakages of personal feeling in otherwise objective designs. It also makes Browning seem more inhibited than he was. Much of his soul-searching through the personal and impersonal dimensions of Art and poetry arose as a natural consequence of the era into which he was born. Such immediate pressures as fidelity to his mother's religiosity were important; more crucial, however, was Browning's instinctive dislike of self-revelatory lyricism as, in himself, a deviant tendency leading him away from the dramatic openness that was more truthful to his own literary temperament. The way in which a poet's instincts grow into mature and confirmed procedures is mysterious; in Browning's rejection of Shelley, he did not dismiss a previous influence so much as announce the nature of what he wanted to achieve.

At this point in his life Browning was incapable of recognizing his own as yet half-formed decisions. *Pippa Passes,* a lyric drama, appeared in 1841. When *Dramatic Lyrics* was published the following year as the third pamphlet in the series of eight *Bells and Pomegranates,* he was still persevering with his ambitious program as a playwright. Included in this small collection were such famous poems as "My Last Duchess," "In a Gondola," and "Porphyria's Lover" (as well as "Rudel to the Lady of Tripoli" and "Christina," with their expressions of idealized, unful-fillable loves and affinities, a belief in the coincidence of souls that probably underlay his impetuous courting of Elizabeth Barrett a few years later). *Dramatic Romances and Lyrics* appeared in November 1845, creating about as little impact as its predecessor.

Since January 10, 1845, however, he had been writing to Elizabeth Barrett and, since May, visiting her at Wimpole Street. Their love correspondence opened with Browning's erotic fan letter. He had just read Barrett's *Poems.* "I do, as I say, love these books with all my heart," he wrote, "and I love you too." He had never set eyes on Elizabeth Barrett, just as the troubadour Rudel had never met the Lady of Tripoli. Barrett's reply made it clear that if Browning's poetry existed in meager circulation, it was cherished by the woman he loved, of whom he knew much but whom he had yet to meet. "Such a letter from such a hand!" she wrote. "Sympathy is dear—very dear to me: but the sympathy of a poet, and such a poet, is the quintessence of sympathy to me."

Browning's next letter brought forth at least a hint of his determination to surpass what he had already identified as his poetic temperament, his challenge to do so issued by his reading of Barrett's *Poems* (1844):

> Your poetry must be, cannot but be, infinitely more to me than mine to you—for you *do* what I always wanted, hoped to do, and only seem now likely to do for the first time. You speak out, *you,*—I only make men and women speak—give you truth bro-ken into prismatic hues, and fear the pure white light, even if it

is in me, but I am going to try; so it will be no small comfort to have your company just now, seeing that when you have your men and women aforesaid, you are busied with them, whereas it seems bleak, melancholy work, this talking to the wind (for I have begun)—yet I don't think I shall let you hear, after all, the savage things about Popes and imaginative religions that I must say.

Mutually supportive criticism might not be the primary gist of the Browning-Barrett love letters; but it is interesting to read Barrett's encouraging answer, defending her future husband against new accusations of obscurity after the appearance of *Dramatic Romances and Lyrics*. It is as if she detected something negative and futile in Browning's hand-wringing, or that she knew enough about his mind to realize that he was blocking his own way forward:

> You have in your vision two worlds, or to use the language of the schools of the day, you are both subjective and objective in the habits of your mind. You can deal both with abstract thought and with human passion in the most passionate sense. Thus, you have an immense grasp in Art; and no one at all accustomed to consider the usual forms of it, could help regarding with reverence and gladness the gradual expansion of your powers. Then you are "masculine" to the height—and I, as a woman, have studied some of your gestures of language and intonation wistfully, as a thing beyond me far! and the more admirable for being beyond.

An extraordinary courtship, elopement, and marriage, their love letters, and Barrett's *Sonnets from the Portuguese* create a story that dominates their biographies with the force of inevitability. It is *the* Victorian love story or else its evergreen popularity makes it appear so. Barrett's unforgiving father, her poor health, her established fame and Browning's aspirations, their flight from England to Italy, first to Pisa, then Florence and their eventual home, Casa Guidi—fiction could not have contrived a better narrative; it has the quality of artistic, amorous, and domestic adventure. But it was neither an uneventful nor a uniformly placid life that the Brownings shared. Two miscarriages were to precede the birth of their son, who was born three days after Mrs. Browning's forty-third birthday. Browning disapproved of how his wife raised the child. He was bewildered by her enthusiasm for spiritualism, and rattled by her eagerness for Louis Napoleon. In the early years of their marriage neither found work congenial. Browning, however, prepared his *Poems* in two volumes, and in 1850 issued *Christmas-Eve and Easter-Day,* which failed to win the readership he might have expected. Throughout his wife's lifetime he was known as "the husband." It fitted in with his understanding of their marriage that he should occupy second place. He identified with a feminine point of view, but although devoted, he was also impractical, without money, and six years younger.

Two such gifted poets, living together but writing from aesthetic principles that were virtually opposed on paper if not in life, could hardly avoid the stimulus of their unusual circumstances and perhaps also an occasional conflict of interests. Elizabeth Barrett Browning set the joint pace with *Casa Guidi Windows* (1851), and from 1853 she was working on her verse novel *Aurora Leigh.* Browning composed *Men and Women,* most of which he seems to have written in about a year; then, with the benefit of second thoughts, or indecision, he postponed publication in order to revise and extend the collection. When it came out late in 1855 he was confronted with many of the same charges that had been leveled at *Sordello.* Bad reviews are discouraging and very often meant to be. Worse, though, is the review (often by the same reviewer) that directs at a markedly different book the same remarks that were pasted on the book before.

Men and Women is now appreciated as a central achievement of the Victorian period and as one of the great books of English poetry. But Browning's poetry was perhaps too concerned with Art for the popularity he craved. It was also indirect in its encounter with contemporary issues, while his characteristic straightness of voice sounded from times and places too distant from average English expectations to win a widespread approval. His exposures of self-deception and love's disillusionment might not have been welcome in an English era that was already buoying itself on a growing, imperial self-confidence often founded on fraudulent emotions and principles that spilled over into domesticity and private conduct.

Self-consciously or not, Browning's cast of mind was nurtured by an almost Elizabethan expansiveness of which his metrical virtuosity can be seen as a technical counterpart. That, and his dramatic method, enabled him to encompass ostensibly out-of-the-way historical or imaginary episodes and their participants with a reanimating vigor and a sentient, intellectual "opulence" (Thomas Carlyle's word). Whatever the blandishments of learning and antiquarianism that drew Browning to at least some of his characters and their situations, these were relegated to minor color-giving roles in his narratives. As an artist he was too submerged in instinctive and intellectual pressures to indulge in the fancy-dress parade of his disguises and mouthpieces. Browning's men and women ignore the obsolete drapery of their former realities to speak in the present reality of their creator's concerns and multiform cadences.

In "One Word More" Browning addresses his wife directly:

> Take them, Love, the book and me together:
> Where the heart lies, let the brain lie also.

There is a feeling of defensiveness as well as assertion in this, the last poem of *Men and Women*. Beneath its surface, like a wise fish aware of the angler on the riverbank, there is a shadowy sensation of unwillingness or regret. His association of feeling and intellect fends off his self-reproach at stepping out of dramatic "objectivity" even for the occasion of a love poem that by any standards is cerebral, and erotic only in its declarations. It is never entirely clear, but he seems to take a pride in impersonality. He might have worded it differently and claimed it was a pride in Art. There is also what comes across as

Browning's relief at having overcome even temporarily the constraints inherent in the fictitious and the dramatic in order to state his love in a poem that concludes the book with the force of a delayed dedication. Critics have found the poem labored and unsatisfactory. I find it audible and affecting. It is certainly a poem that Browning wrote against his own grain while wishing that were not so—hence its under-the-surface turbulence.

Raphael's love sonnets have vanished "as rare things will," Dante's attempted angel-painting was ruined by the intervention of "people of importance." "What of Rafael's sonnets, Dante's picture?" Browning asks, looking for his clearance in precedents he considered honorable and artistic:

> This: no artist lives and loves, that longs not
> Once, and only once, and for one only,
> (Ah, the prize!) to find his love a language
> Fit and fair and simple and sufficient—
> Using nature that's an art to others,
> Not, this one time, art that's turned his nature.

"Art that's turned his nature"? Browning might have resented his temperamental preference for fiction and, at the same time, remained supremely self-aware of artifice to the point that he distrusted the "personal" in poetry outside the "Once, and only once, and for one only," or what he implies is a moment of necessary self-revelation. He even seems to suggest that autobiographical and dramatic utterance are as unlike each other as Raphael's recourse to poetry, or Dante's to painting, that he is stepping out of one Art into another:

> Ay, of all the artists living, loving,
> None but would forego his proper dowry,—
> Does he paint? he fain would write a poem,—
> Does he write? he fain would paint a picture,
> Put to proof art alien to the artist's,

> *Once, and only once, and for one only,*
> *So to be the man and leave the artist,*
> *Gain the man's joy, miss the artist's sorrow.*

Or, as he says later, "He who writes, may write for once as I do." It can seem anything other than a poem of love; but it *is* a love poem, in which all that is meant by love is gestured through the devotion implicated as a cause of Browning's momentary reversal of his aesthetic beliefs, his putting to the proof "art alien to the artist's." Cerebral and austere as it might seem, the gesture is affecting, and feeling is heightened by his refusal to abdicate intelligence—"Where my heart lies, let my brain lie also!"

> *God be thanked, the meanest of his creatures*
> *Boasts two soul-sides, one to face the world with,*
> *One to show a woman when he loves her!*

In *Sordello* Browning wrote of "Man-portion" and "Poet-part," and "The Poet thwarting hopelessly the man." "Often lyric in expression, always Dramatic in principle," he wrote firmly of his poetry, "and so many utterances of so many imaginary persons, not mine." Early experiences dating back to *Pauline* chastened him to avoid the publication of personal emotion, but it is preposterous to describe so voluminous a writer as reticent even if he was taciturn in the face of public prying. Man and Poet were different natures to Browning and his poetic served to establish a working arrangement between them, not their severance. At one time his dramatic procedures might have recommended themselves to him as a means to relegate personality and self, but it is clear from the poetry itself—mettlesome, adventurous, speculative—that they introduced imaginative risks as much as they obviated the need for personal disclosures.

Nowhere is that clearer than in "Childe Roland to the Dark Tower Came." Somber and symphonic, its effect such as to remind us of

Wordsworth's phrase "the visionary dreariness," the poem unfolds a mood and landscape of endurance and failure, of quest, fidelity, arrival, and recognition. It is Browning's masterpiece, perhaps; I would feel more confident were it not that several others of his poems are equally magnificent in their imaginative performance, but of different kinds. "Andrea del Sarto" and "Fra Lippo Lippi" are examples. In "One Word More" he wrote of finding a language for that occasion, "Fit and fair and simple and sufficient." In so much of Browning's poetry, forms, meters, diction, and vocabulary search for a unique fittingness, a voicing of poetry "once, and only once," for that poem only. It illustrates his astounding scrupulousness and artistic integrity, which will always be a challenge to those who read him. It shows too the degree to which he insisted to himself that instinct and feeling should collaborate with intelligence and hammer out the matter between them.

Too fastidious and hygienic an approach to the writing of poetry? There are times when it feels appropriate to say yes, times when it seems hardly credible that a poet's temperament should be as alert as Browning's to human occasions and psychologies and yet remain so suspicious and even contemptuous of his own events. Yet it is very likely that Browning's temperament was like that; it seems possible that his dislike of autobiography was bluster born of an embarrassment that "the pure white light" he admired in his wife's poetry—"my moon of poets," he called her— and in others' poetry, was absent among his otherwise lavish gifts. Browning's poetry is admirable in its *impure* dazzle and radiance, its taint of life—life itself, as I would claim, not Browning's own necessarily limited experience, but fiction's travels and a mind made audible through a full-throated range of vocabulary and meters; life dipped in language by a wholehearted man and, for the most part, spoken by his characters in a way that creates the presence of Browning engaging with truth and art at an uncompromising level of seriousness.

"It is easy to cage the poet bird," Yeats's father wrote him in a letter. "Tennyson was caught and as for Browning he was born in a cage."

It is too glib and easy a dismissal and disregards too much. It presupposes that Browning did not know what he was doing or that he was unaware of subjective leakages in his poetry, or that he was unconscious of the coincidences of fiction and life, or that he failed to observe where his own thoughts and feelings overlapped or diverged from those he ascribed to his speakers. His astute, sometimes hair-raising, ironies testify to more than the theatricality of his imagination; they indicate a mind that was attentive to its own characteristic strategies, the intrigues it conducted with itself in order to overcome personality and its limitations.

His temperament demanded that he withdraw from his private sorrows, affections, joys, and immediate day-to-day concerns, but it can be supposed that a poet of Browning's intellect could observe his imagination at work, and know that his quotidian negatives and positives would inform his fictitious designs. In all likelihood, he would, as an artist, be delighted in their *deserved* occurrences, knowing that fiction about men and women is unresolved in its objectivity, because it is written by men and women.

A measure of his temperament is gained by his reply to the question why he never wrote personal commemorative elegiac poetry: "In the two or three great sorrows of my life, it has been the last thing that occurred to me." Here his bluster is sad but true; we can take his word for it while suspecting that it *did* occur to a poet as sapient as Browning was. It is too much to believe that he wrote "James Lee's Wife" without sensing its mood, or that he was unconscious of the fictitious, erotic remorse of "Too Late." He wrote *about,* and around, his feelings.

Selecting from Browning has at times felt like an act of impertinence. Some standard anthology pieces are missing in order to make room for what I considered "essential." There has been no room for dramatic poems on a larger scale such as "Bishop Brougham's Apology" or "Mr. Sludge, the Medium," nor have I thought it permissible to abbreviate them or *Sordello* or *The Ring and the Book.* Many of the selections come from *Men and Women,* for which no apology need be made.

It is a commonplace that as he aged Browning became an optimistic bore and a would-be cleanser of cobwebs, with a consequent youthful senility in his work. It is far from the truth, and I have included "Numpholeptos," "At the 'Mermaid'," "Pan and Luna," and the opening passages of *La Saisiaz* to prove it. Thomas Hardy's opinion, however, is still one to consider: "The longer I live, the more does Browning's character seem *the* literary puzzle of the 19th century." He was thinking of the dissonance between Browning the poet and Browning the public figure who looked and behaved not at all as it was expected he should. Henry James, perhaps a more avid diner-out than Browning himself, recorded the emptiness of Browning's table talk, his "shrill interruptingness." "Evidently," James wrote to his sister, Alice, "there are two Brownings—an esoteric and an exoteric. The former never peeps out in society, and the latter has not a suggestion of *Men and Women.*" Browning, though, meant more to James than a disappointment at a London dinner party. He was a poet of "large liberty and free experiment," his work a wonderful mixture of "the universal and the alembicated." He was also "the writer of our time of whom, in the face of the rest of the world, the English tongue may be most proud—for he has touched *every*thing, and with a breadth!"

—DOUGLAS DUNN

Poems

FROM *DRAMATIC LYRICS,* 1842

My Last Duchess

FERRARA

That's my last Duchess painted on the wall,
Looking as if she were alive. I call
That piece a wonder, now: Frà Pandolf's hands
Worked busily a day, and there she stands.
Will't please you sit and look at her? I said
"Frà Pandolf" by design, for never read
Strangers like you that pictured countenance,
The depth and passion of its earnest glance,
But to myself they turned (since none puts by
The curtain I have drawn for you, but I)
And seemed as they would ask me, if they durst,
How such a glance came there; so, not the first
Are you to turn and ask thus. Sir, 'twas not
Her husband's presence only, called that spot
Of joy into the Duchess' cheek: perhaps
Frà Pandolf chanced to say "Her mantle laps
Over my lady's wrist too much," or "Paint
Must never hope to reproduce the faint
Half-flush that dies along her throat": such stuff
Was courtesy, she thought, and cause enough
For calling up that spot of joy. She had

A heart—how shall I say?—too soon made glad,
Too easily impressed; she liked whate'er
She looked on, and her looks went everywhere.
Sir, 'twas all one! My favour at her breast,
The dropping of the daylight in the West,
The bough of cherries some officious fool
Broke in the orchard for her, the white mule
She rode with round the terrace—all and each
Would draw from her alike the approving speech,
Or blush, at least. She thanked men,—good! but thanked
Somehow—I know not how—as if she ranked
My gift of a nine-hundred-years-old name
With anybody's gift. Who'd stoop to blame
This sort of trifling? Even had you skill
In speech—(which I have not)—to make your will
Quite clear to such an one, and say, "Just this
Or that in you disgusts me; here you miss,
Or there exceed the mark"—and if she let
Herself be lessoned so, nor plainly set
Her wits to yours, forsooth, and made excuse,
—E'en then would be some stooping; and I choose
Never to stoop. Oh sir, she smiled, no doubt,
Whene'er I passed her; but who passed without
Much the same smile? This grew; I gave commands;
Then all smiles stopped together. There she stands
As if alive. Will't please you rise? We'll meet
The company below, then. I repeat,
The Count your master's known munificence
Is ample warrant that no just pretence
Of mine for dowry will be disallowed;
Though his fair daughter's self, as I avowed
At starting, is my object. Nay, we'll go
Together down, sir. Notice Neptune, though,
Taming a sea-horse, thought a rarity,
Which Claus of Innsbruck cast in bronze for me!

Porphyria's Lover

The rain set early in tonight,
   The sullen wind was soon awake,
It tore the elm-tops down for spite,
   And did its worst to vex the lake:
   I listened with heart fit to break.
When glided in Porphyria; straight
   She shut the cold out and the storm,
And kneeled and made the cheerless grate
   Blaze up, and all the cottage warm;
   Which done, she rose, and from her form
Withdrew the dripping cloak and shawl,
   And laid her soiled gloves by, untied
Her hat and let the damp hair fall,
   And, last, she sat down by my side
   And called me. When no voice replied,
She put my arm about her waist,
   And made her smooth white shoulder bare,
And all her yellow hair displaced,
   And, stooping, made my cheek lie there,
   And spread, o'er all, her yellow hair,
Murmuring how she loved me—she
   Too weak, for all her heart's endeavour,
To set its struggling passion free
   From pride, and vainer ties dissever,
   And give herself to me for ever.
But passion sometimes would prevail,
   Nor could tonight's gay feast restrain
A sudden thought of one so pale
   For love of her, and all in vain:
   So, she was come through wind and rain.
Be sure I looked up at her eyes
   Happy and proud; at last I knew
Porphyria worshipped me; surprise

Made my heart swell, and still it grew
While I debated what to do.
That moment she was mine, mine, fair,
Perfectly pure and good: I found
A thing to do, and all her hair
In one long yellow string I wound
Three times her little throat around,
And strangled her. No pain felt she;
I am quite sure she felt no pain.
As a shut bud that holds a bee,
I warily oped her lids: again
Laughed the blue eyes without a stain.
And I untightened next the tress
About her neck; her cheek once more
Blushed bright beneath my burning kiss:
I propped her head up as before,
Only, this time my shoulder bore
Her head, which droops upon it still:
The smiling rosy little head,
So glad it has its utmost will,
That all it scorned at once is fled,
And I, its love, am gained instead!
Porphyria's love: she guessed not how
Her darling one wish would be heard.
And thus we sit together now,
And all night long we have not stirred,
And yet God has not said a word!

FROM *DRAMATIC ROMANCES AND LYRICS,*
1845

The Lost Leader

I

Just for a handful of silver he left us,
   Just for a riband to stick in his coat—
Found the one gift of which fortune bereft us,
   Lost all the others she lets us devote;
They, with the gold to give, doled him out silver,
   So much was theirs who so little allowed:
How all our copper had gone for his service!
   Rags—were they purple, his heart had been proud!
We that had loved him so, followed him, honoured him,
   Lived in his mild and magnificent eye,
Learned his great language, caught his clear accents,
   Made him our pattern to live and to die!
Shakespeare was of us, Milton was for us,
   Burns, Shelley, were with us,—they watch from their graves!
He alone breaks from the van and the freemen,
   —He alone sinks to the rear and the slaves!

II

We shall march prospering,—not through his presence;
   Songs may inspirit us,—not from his lyre;
Deeds will be done,—while he boasts his quiescence,
   Still bidding crouch whom the rest bade aspire:
Blot out his name, then, record one lost soul more,
   One task more declined, one more footpath untrod,
One more devils'-triumph and sorrow for angels,
   One wrong more to man, one more insult to God!
Life's night begins: let him never come back to us!
   There would be doubt, hesitation and pain,

Forced praise on our part—the glimmer of twilight,
    Never glad confident morning again!
Best fight on well, for we taught him—strike gallantly,
    Menace our heart ere we master his own;
Then let him receive the new knowledge and wait us,
    Pardoned in heaven, the first by the throne!

Home-Thoughts, from Abroad

I

Oh, to be in England
Now that April's there,
And whoever wakes in England
Sees, some morning, unaware,
That the lowest boughs and the brushwood sheaf
Round the elm-tree bole are in tiny leaf,
While the chaffinch sings on the orchard bough
In England—now!

II

And after April, when May follows,
And the whitethroat builds, and all the swallows!
Hark, where my blossomed pear-tree in the hedge
Leans to the field and scatters on the clover
Blossoms and dewdrops—at the bent spray's edge—
That's the wise thrush; he sings each song twice over,
Lest you should think he never could recapture
The first fine careless rapture!
And though the fields look rough with hoary dew,
All will be gay when noontide wakes anew
The buttercups, the little children's dower
—Far brighter than this gaudy melon-flower!

The Bishop Orders His Tomb at Saint Praxed's Church

ROME, 15—

Vanity, saith the preacher, vanity!
Draw round my bed: is Anselm keeping back?
Nephews—sons mine . . . ah God, I know not! Well—
She, men would have to be your mother once,
Old Gandolf envied me, so fair she was!
What's done is done, and she is dead beside,
Dead long ago, and I am Bishop since,
And as she died so must we die ourselves,
And thence ye may perceive the world's a dream.
Life, how and what is it? As here I lie
In this state-chamber, dying by degrees,
Hours and long hours in the dead night, I ask
"Do I live, am I dead?" Peace, peace seems all.
Saint Praxed's ever was the church for peace;
And so, about this tomb of mine. I fought
With tooth and nail to save my niche, ye know:
—Old Gandolf cozened me, despite my care;
Shrewd was that snatch from out the corner South
He graced his carrion with, God curse the same!
Yet still my niche is not so cramped but thence
One sees the pulpit o' the epistle-side,
And somewhat of the choir, those silent seats,
And up into the airy dome where live
The angels, and a sunbeam's sure to lurk:
And I shall fill my slab of basalt there,
And 'neath my tabernacle take my rest,
With those nine columns round me, two and two,
The odd one at my feet where Anselm stands:
Peach-blossom marble all, the rare, the ripe
As fresh-poured red wine of a mighty pulse.

—Old Gandolf with his paltry onion-stone,
Put me where I may look at him! True peach,
Rosy and flawless: how I earned the prize!
Draw close: that conflagration of my church
—What then? So much was saved if aught were missed!
My sons, ye would not be my death? Go dig
The white-grape vineyard where the oil-press stood,
Drop water gently till the surface sink,
And if ye find . . . Ah God, I know not, I! . . .
Bedded in store of rotten fig-leaves soft,
And corded up in a tight olive-frail,
Some lump, ah God, of *lapis lazuli,*
Big as a Jew's head cut off at the nape,
Blue as a vein o'er the Madonna's breast . . .
Sons, all have I bequeathed you, villas, all,
That brave Frascati villa with its bath,
So, let the blue lump poise between my knees,
Like God the Father's globe on both his hands
Ye worship in the Jesu Church so gay,
For Gandolf shall not choose but see and burst!
Swift as a weaver's shuttle fleet our years:
Man goeth to the grave, and where is he?
Did I say basalt for my slab, sons? Black—
'Twas ever antique-black I meant! How else
Shall ye contrast my frieze to come beneath?
The bas-relief in bronze ye promised me,
Those Pans and Nymphs ye wot of, and perchance
Some tripod, thyrsus, with a vase or so,
The Saviour at his sermon on the mount,
Saint Praxed in a glory, and one Pan
Ready to twitch the Nymph's last garment off,
And Moses with the tables . . . but I know
Ye mark me not! What do they whisper thee,
Child of my bowels, Anselm? Ah, ye hope

To revel down my villas while I gasp
Bricked o'er with beggar's mouldy travertine
Which Gandolf from his tomb-top chuckles at!
Nay, boys, ye love me—all of jasper, then!
'Tis jasper ye stand pledged to, lest I grieve
My bath must needs be left behind, alas!
One block, pure green as a pistachio-nut,
There's plenty jasper somewhere in the world—
And have I not Saint Praxed's ear to pray
Horses for ye, and brown Greek manuscripts,
And mistresses with great smooth marbly limbs?
—That's if ye carve my epitaph aright,
Choice Latin, picked phrase, Tully's every word,
No gaudy ware like Gandolf's second line—
Tully, my masters? Ulpian serves his need!
And then how I shall lie through centuries,
And hear the blessed mutter of the mass,
And see God made and eaten all day long,
And feel the steady candle-flame, and taste
Good strong thick stupefying incense-smoke!
For as I lie here, hours of the dead night,
Dying in state and by such slow degrees,
I fold my arms as if they clasped a crook,
And stretch my feet forth straight as stone can point,
And let the bedclothes, for a mortcloth, drop
Into great laps and folds of sculptor's-work:
And as yon tapers dwindle, and strange thoughts
Grow, with a certain humming in my ears,
About the life before I lived this life,
And this life too, popes, cardinals and priests,
Saint Praxed at his sermon on the mount,
Your tall pale mother with her talking eyes,
And new-found agate urns as fresh as day,
And marble's language, Latin pure, discreet,

—Aha, ELUCESCEBAT quoth our friend?
No Tully, said I, Ulpian at the best!
Evil and brief hath been my pilgrimage.
All *lapis,* all, sons! Else I give the Pope
My villas! Will ye ever eat my heart?
Ever your eyes were as a lizard's quick,
They glitter like your mother's for my soul,
Or ye would heighten my impoverished frieze,
Piece out its starved design, and fill my vase
With grapes, and add a vizor and a Term,
And to the tripod ye would tie a lynx
That in his struggle throws the thyrsus down,
To comfort me on my entablature
Whereon I am to lie till I must ask
"Do I live, am I dead?" There, leave me, there!
For ye have stabbed me with ingratitude
To death—ye wish it—God, ye wish it! Stone—
Gritstone, a-crumble! Clammy squares which sweat
As if the corpse they keep were oozing through—
And no more *lapis* to delight the world!
Well go! I bless ye. Fewer tapers there,
But in a row: and, going, turn your backs
—Ay, like departing altar-ministrants,
And leave me in my church, the church for peace,
That I may watch at leisure if he leers—
Old Gandolf, at me, from his onion-stone,
As still he envied me, so fair she was!

Meeting at Night

I

The grey sea and the long black land;
And the yellow half-moon large and low;
And the startled little waves that leap

In fiery ringlets from their sleep,
As I gain the cove with pushing prow,
And quench its speed i' the slushy sand.

II

Then a mile of warm sea-scented beach;
Three fields to cross till a farm appears;
A tap at the pane, the quick sharp scratch
And blue spurt of a lighted match,
And a voice less loud, through its joys and fears,
Than the two hearts beating each to each!

FROM *MEN AND WOMEN,* 1855

Love Among the Ruins

I

Where the quiet-coloured end of evening smiles,
  Miles and miles
On the solitary pastures where our sheep
  Half-asleep
Tinkle homeward through the twilight, stray or stop
  As they crop—
Was the site once of a city great and gay,
  (So they say)
Of our country's very capital, its prince
  Ages since
Held his court in, gathered councils, wielding far
  Peace or war.

II

Now,—the country does not even boast a tree,
  As you see,

To distinguish slopes of verdure, certain rills
    From the hills
Intersect and give a name to, (else they run
    Into one)
Where the domed and daring palace shot its spires
    Up like fires
O'er the hundred-gated circuit of a wall
    Bounding all,
Made of marble, men might march on nor be pressed,
    Twelve abreast.

III

And such plenty and perfection, see, of grass
    Never was!
Such a carpet as, this summer-time, o'erspreads
    And embeds
Every vestige of the city, guessed alone,
    Stock or stone—
Where a multitude of men breathed joy and woe
    Long ago;
Lust of glory pricked their hearts up, dread of shame
    Struck them tame;
And that glory and that shame alike, the gold
    Bought and sold.

IV

Now,—the single little turret that remains
    On the plains,
By the caper over-rooted, by the gourd
    Overscored,
While the patching houseleek's head of blossom winks
    Through the chinks—
Marks the basement whence a tower in ancient time
    Sprang sublime,

And a burning ring, all round, the chariots traced
    As they raced,
And the monarch and his minions and his dames
    Viewed the games.

V

And I know, while thus the quiet-coloured eve
    Smiles to leave
To their folding, all our many-tinkling fleece
    In such peace,
And the slopes and rills in undistinguished grey
    Melt away—
That a girl with eager eyes and yellow hair
    Waits me there
In the turret whence the charioteers caught soul
    For the goal,
When the king looked, where she looks now, breathless, dumb
    Till I come.

VI

But he looked upon the city, every side,
    Far and wide,
All the mountains topped with temples, all the glades'
    Colonnades,
All the causeys, bridges, aqueducts,—and then,
    All the men!
When I do come, she will speak not, she will stand,
    Either hand
On my shoulder, give her eyes the first embrace
    Of my face,
Ere we rush, ere we extinguish sight and speech
    Each on each.

VII

In one year they sent a million fighters forth
　　South and North,
And they built their gods a brazen pillar high
　　As the sky,
Yet reserved a thousand chariots in full force—
　　Gold, of course.
Oh heart! oh blood that freezes, blood that burns!
　　Earth's returns
For whole centuries of folly, noise and sin!
　　Shut them in,
With their triumphs and their glories and the rest!
　　Love is best.

Evelyn Hope

I

Beautiful Evelyn Hope is dead!
　　Sit and watch by her side an hour.
That is her book-shelf, this her bed;
　　She plucked that piece of geranium-flower,
Beginning to die too, in the glass;
　　Little has yet been changed, I think:
The shutters are shut, no light may pass
　　Save two long rays through the hinge's chink.

II

Sixteen years old when she died!
　　Perhaps she had scarcely heard my name;
It was not her time to love; beside,
　　Her life had many a hope and aim,
Duties enough and little cares,
　　And now was quiet, now astir,
Till God's hand beckoned unawares,—
　　And the sweet white brow is all of her.

III

Is it too late then, Evelyn Hope?
　　What, your soul was pure and true,
The good stars met in your horoscope,
　　Made you of spirit, fire and dew—
And, just because I was thrice as old
　　And our paths in the world diverged so wide,
Each was naught to each, must I be told?
　　We were fellow mortals, naught beside?

IV

No, indeed! for God above
　　Is great to grant, as mighty to make,
And creates the love to reward the love:
　　I claim you still, for my own love's sake!
Delayed it may be for more lives yet,
　　Through worlds I shall traverse, not a few:
Much is to learn, much to forget
　　Ere the time be come for taking you.

V

But the time will come,—at last it will,
　　When, Evelyn Hope, what meant (I shall say)
In the lower earth, in the years long still,
　　That body and soul so pure and gay?
Why your hair was amber, I shall divine,
　　And your mouth of your own geranium's red—
And what you would do with me, in fine,
　　In the new life come in the old one's stead.

VI

I have lived (I shall say) so much since then,
　　Given up myself so many times,
Gained me the gains of various men,
　　Ransacked the ages, spoiled the climes;

Yet one thing, one, in my soul's full scope,
    Either I missed or itself missed me:
And I want and find you, Evelyn Hope!
    What is the issue? let us see!

VII

I loved you, Evelyn, all the while.
    My heart seemed full as it could hold?
There was place and to spare for the frank young smile,
    And the red young mouth, and the hair's young gold.
So, hush,—I will give you this leaf to keep:
    See, I shut it inside the sweet cold hand!
There, that is our secret: go to sleep!
    You will wake, and remember, and understand.

Fra Lippo Lippi

I am poor brother Lippo, by your leave!
You need not clap your torches to my face.
Zooks, what's to blame? you think you see a monk!
What, 'tis past midnight, and you go the rounds,
And here you catch me at an alley's end
Where sportive ladies leave their doors ajar?
The Carmine's my cloister: hunt it up,
Do,—harry out, if you must show your zeal,
Whatever rat, there, haps on his wrong hole,
And nip each softling of a wee white mouse,
Weke, weke, that's crept to keep him company!
Aha, you know your betters! Then, you'll take
Your hand away that's fiddling on my throat,
And please to know me likewise. Who am I?
Why, one, sir, who is lodging with a friend
Three streets off—he's a certain . . . how d'ye call?
Master—a . . . Cosimo of the Medici,

I' the house that caps the corner. Boh! you were best!
Remember and tell me, the day you're hanged,
How you affected such a gullet's-gripe!
But you, sir, it concerns you that your knaves
Pick up a manner nor discredit you:
Zooks, are we pilchards, that they sweep the streets
And count fair prize what comes into their net?
He's Judas to a tittle, that man is!
Just such a face! Why, sir, you make amends.
Lord, I'm not angry! Bid your hangdogs go
Drink out this quarter-florin to the health
Of the munificent House that harbours me
(And many more beside, lads! more beside!)
And all's come square again. I'd like his face—
His, elbowing on his comrade in the door
With the pike and lantern,—for the slave that holds
John Baptist's head a-dangle by the hair
With one hand ("Look you, now," as who should say)
And his weapon in the other, yet unwiped!
It's not your chance to have a bit of chalk,
A wood-coal or the like? or you should see!
Yes, I'm the painter, since you style me so.
What, brother Lippo's doings, up and down,
You know them and they take you? like enough!
I saw the proper twinkle in your eye—
'Tell you, I liked your looks at very first.
Let's sit and set things straight now, hip to haunch.
Here's spring come, and the nights one makes up bands
To roam the town and sing out carnival,
And I've been three weeks shut within my mew,
A-painting for the great man, saints and saints
And saints again. I could not paint all night—
Ouf! I leaned out of window for fresh air.
There came a hurry of feet and little feet,

A sweep of lute-strings, laughs, and whifs of song,—
Flower o' the broom,
Take away love, and our earth is a tomb!
Flower o' the quince,
I let Lisa go, and what good in life since?
Flower o' the thyme—and so on. Round they went.
Scarce had they turned the corner when a titter
Like the skipping of rabbits by moonlight,—three slim shapes,
And a face that looked up . . . zooks, sir, flesh and blood,
That's all I'm made of! Into shreds it went,
Curtain and counterpane and coverlet,
All the bed-furniture—a dozen knots,
There was a ladder! Down I let myself,
Hands and feet, scrambling somehow, and so dropped,
And after them. I came up with the fun
Hard by Saint Laurence, hail fellow, well met,—
Flower o' the rose,
If I've been merry, what matter who knows?
And so as I was stealing back again
To get to bed and have a bit of sleep
Ere I rise up tomorrow and go work
On Jerome knocking at his poor old breast
With his great round stone to subdue the flesh,
You snap me of the sudden. Ah, I see!
Though your eye twinkles still, you shake your head—
Mine's shaved—a monk, you say—the sting's in that!
If Master Cosimo announced himself,
Mum's the word naturally; but a monk!
Come, what am I a beast for? tell us, now!
I was a baby when my mother died
And father died and left me in the street.
I starved there, God knows how, a year or two
On fig-skins, melon-parings, rinds and shucks,
Refuse and rubbish. One fine frosty day,

My stomach being empty as your hat,
The wind doubled me up and down I went.
Old Aunt Lapaccia trussed me with one hand,
(Its fellow was a stinger as I knew)
And so along the wall, over the bridge,
By the straight cut to the convent. Six words there,
While I stood munching my first bread that month:
"So, boy, you're minded," quoth the good fat father
Wiping his own mouth, 'twas refection-time,—
"To quit this very miserable world?
Will you renounce" . . . "the mouthful of bread?" thought I;
By no means! Brief, they made a monk of me;
I did renounce the world, its pride and greed,
Palace, farm, villa, shop and banking-house,
Trash, such as these poor devils of Medici
Have given their hearts to—all at eight years old.
Well, sir, I found in time, you may be sure,
'Twas not for nothing—the good bellyful,
The warm serge and the rope that goes all round,
And day-long blessed idleness beside!
"Let's see what the urchin's fit for"—that came next.
Not overmuch their way, I must confess.
Such a to-do! They tried me with their books:
Lord, they'd have taught me Latin in pure waste!
Flower o' the clove,
All the Latin I construe is, "amo" I love!
But, mind you, when a boy starves in the streets
Eight years together, as my fortune was,
Watching folk's faces to know who will fling
The bit of half-stripped grape-bunch he desires,
And who will curse or kick him for his pains,—
Which gentleman processional and fine,
Holding a candle to the Sacrament,
Will wink and let him lift a plate and catch

The droppings of the wax to sell again,
Or holla for the Eight and have him whipped,—
How say I?—nay, which dog bites, which lets drop
His bone from the heap of offal in the street,—
Why, soul and sense of him grow sharp alike,
He learns the look of things, and none the less
For admonition from the hunger-pinch.
I had a store of such remarks, be sure,
Which, after I found leisure, turned to use.
I drew men's faces on my copy-books,
Scrawled them within the antiphonary's marge,
Joined legs and arms to the long music-notes,
Found eyes and nose and chin for A's and B's,
And made a string of pictures of the world
Betwixt the ins and outs of verb and noun,
On the wall, the bench, the door. The monks looked black.
"Nay," quoth the Prior, "turn him out, d'ye say?
In no wise. Lose a crow and catch a lark.
What if at last we get our man of parts,
We Carmelites, like those Camaldolese
And Preaching Friars, to do our church up fine
And put the front on it that ought to be!"
And hereupon he bade me daub away.
Thank you! my head being crammed, the walls a blank,
Never was such prompt disemburdening.
First, every sort of monk, the black and white,
I drew them, fat and lean: then, folk at church,
From good old gossips waiting to confess
Their cribs of barrel-droppings, candle-ends,—
To the breathless fellow at the altar-foot,
Fresh from his murder, safe and sitting there
With the little children round him in a row
Of admiration, half for his beard and half
For that white anger of his victim's son

Shaking a fist at him with one fierce arm,
Signing himself with the other because of Christ
(Whose sad face on the cross sees only this
After the passion of a thousand years)
Till some poor girl, her apron o'er her head,
(Which the intense eyes looked through) came at eve
On tiptoe, said a word, dropped in a loaf,
Her pair of earrings and a bunch of flowers
(The brute took growling), prayed, and so was gone.
I painted all, then cried " 'Tis ask and have;
Choose, for more's ready!"—laid the ladder flat,
And showed my covered bit of cloister-wall.
The monks closed in a circle and praised loud
Till checked, taught what to see and not to see,
Being simple bodies,—"That's the very man!
Look at the boy who stoops to pat the dog!
That woman's like the Prior's niece who comes
To care about his asthma: it's the life!"
But there my triumph's straw-fire flared and funked;
Their betters took their turn to see and say:
The Prior and the learned pulled a face
And stopped all that in no time. "How? what's here?
Quite from the mark of painting, bless us all!
Faces, arms, legs and bodies like the true
As much as pea and pea! it's devil's-game!
Your business is not to catch men with show,
With homage to the perishable clay,
But lift them over it, ignore it all,
Make them forget there's such a thing as flesh.
Your business is to paint the souls of men—
Man's soul, and it's a fire, smoke . . . no, it's not . . .
It's vapour done up like a new-born babe—
(In that shape when you die it leaves your mouth)
It's . . . well, what matters talking, it's the soul!

Give us no more of body than shows soul!
Here's Giotto, with his Saint a-praising God,
That sets us praising,—why not stop with him?
Why put all thoughts of praise out of our head
With wonder at lines, colours, and what not?
Paint the soul, never mind the legs and arms!
Rub all out, try at it a second time.
Oh, that white smallish female with the breasts,
She's just my niece . . . Herodias, I would say,—
Who went and danced and got men's heads cut off!
Have it all out!" Now, is this sense, I ask?
A fine way to paint soul, by painting body
So ill, the eye can't stop there, must go further
And can't fare worse! Thus, yellow does for white
When what you put for yellow's simply black,
And any sort of meaning looks intense
When all beside itself means and looks naught.
Why can't a painter lift each foot in turn,
Left foot and right foot, go a double step,
Make his flesh liker and his soul more like,
Both in their order? Take the prettiest face,
The Prior's niece . . . patron-saint—is it so pretty
You can't discover if it means hope, fear,
Sorrow or joy? won't beauty go with these?
Suppose I've made her eyes all right and blue,
Can't I take breath and try to add life's flash,
And then add soul and heighten them threefold?
Or say there's beauty with no soul at all—
(I never saw it—put the case the same—)
If you get simple beauty and naught else,
You get about the best thing God invents:
That's somewhat: and you'll find the soul you have missed,
Within yourself, when you return him thanks.
"Rub all out!" Well, well, there's my life, in short,

And so the thing has gone on ever since.
I'm grown a man no doubt, I've broken bounds:
You should not take a fellow eight years old
And make him swear to never kiss the girls.
I'm my own master, paint now as I please—
Having a friend, you see, in the Corner-house!
Lord, it's fast holding by the rings in front—
Those great rings serve more purposes than just
To plant a flag in, or tie up a horse!
And yet the old schooling sticks, the old grave eyes
Are peeping o'er my shoulder as I work,
The heads shake still—"It's art's decline, my son!
You're not of the true painters, great and old;
Brother Angelico's the man, you'll find;
Brother Lorenzo stands his single peer:
Fag on at flesh, you'll never make the third!"
Flower o' the pine,
You keep your mistr . . . manners, and I'll stick to mine!
I'm not the third, then: bless us, they must know!
Don't you think they're the likeliest to know,
They with their Latin? So, I swallow my rage,
Clench my teeth, suck my lips in tight, and paint
To please them—sometimes do and sometimes don't;
For, doing most, there's pretty sure to come
A turn, some warm eve finds me at my saints—
A laugh, a cry, the business of the world—
(*Flower o' the peach,*
Death for us all, and his own life for each!)
And my whole soul revolves, the cup runs over,
The world and life's too big to pass for a dream,
And I do these wild things in sheer despite,
And play the fooleries you catch me at,
In pure rage! The old mill-horse, out at grass
After hard years, throws up his stiff heels so,

Although the miller does not preach to him
The only good of grass is to make chaff.
What would men have? Do they like grass or no—
May they or mayn't they? all I want's the thing
Settled for ever one way. As it is,
You tell too many lies and hurt yourself:
You don't like what you only like too much,
You do like what, if given you at your word,
You find abundantly detestable.
For me, I think I speak as I was taught;
I always see the garden and God there
A-making man's wife: and, my lesson learned,
The value and significance of flesh,
I can't unlearn ten minutes afterwards.

You understand me: I'm a beast, I know.
But see, now—why, I see as certainly
As that the morning-star's about to shine,
What will hap some day. We've a youngster here
Comes to our convent, studies what I do,
Slouches and stares and lets no atom drop:
His name is Guidi—he'll not mind the monks—
They call him Hulking Tom, he lets them talk—
He picks my practice up—he'll paint apace,
I hope so—though I never live so long,
I know what's sure to follow. You be judge!
You speak no Latin more than I, belike;
However, you're my man, you've seen the world
—The beauty and the wonder and the power,
The shapes of things, their colours, lights and shades,
Changes, surprises—and God made it all!
—For what? Do you feel thankful, ay or no,
For this fair town's face, yonder river's line,
The mountain round it and the sky above,

Much more the figures of man, woman, child,
These are the frame to? What's it all about?
To be passed over, despised? or dwelt upon,
Wondered at? oh, this last of course!—you say.
But why not do as well as say,—paint these
Just as they are, careless what comes of it?
God's works—paint anyone, and count it crime
To let a truth slip. Don't object, "His works
Are here already; nature is complete:
Suppose you reproduce her"—(which you can't)
"There's no advantage! you must beat her, then."
For, don't you mark? we're made so that we love
First when we see them painted, things we have passed
Perhaps a hundred times nor cared to see;
And so they are better, painted—better to us,
Which is the same thing. Art was given for that;
God uses us to help each other so,
Lending our minds out. Have you noticed, now,
Your cullion's hanging face? A bit of chalk,
And trust me but you should, though! How much more,
If I drew higher things with the same truth!
That were to take the Prior's pulpit-place,
Interpret God to all of you! Oh, oh,
It makes me mad to see what men shall do
And we in our graves! This world's no blot for us,
Nor blank; it means intensely, and means good:
To find its meaning is my meat and drink.
"Ay, but you don't so instigate to prayer!"
Strikes in the Prior: "when your meaning's plain
It does not say to folk—remember matins,
Or, mind you fast next Friday!" Why, for this
What need of art at all? A skull and bones,
Two bits of stick nailed crosswise, or, what's best,
A bell to chime the hour with, does as well.

I painted a Saint Laurence six months since
At Prato, splashed the fresco in fine style:
"How looks my painting, now the scaffold's down?"
I ask a brother: "Hugely," he returns—
"Already not one phiz of your three slaves
Who turn the Deacon off his toasted side,
But's scratched and prodded to our heart's content,
The pious people have so eased their own
With coming to say prayers there in a rage:
We get on fast to see the bricks beneath.
Expect another job this time next year,
For pity and religion grow i' the crowd—
Your painting serves its purpose!" Hang the fools!

    —That is—you'll not mistake an idle word
Spoke in a huff by a poor monk, Got wot,
Tasting the air this spicy night which turns
The unaccustomed head like Chianti wine!
Oh, the church knows! don't misreport me, now!
It's natural a poor monk out of bounds
Should have his apt word to excuse himself:
And hearken how I plot to make amends.
I have bethought me: I shall paint a piece
. . . There's for you! Give me six months, then go, see
Something in Sant' Ambrogio's! Bless the nuns!
They want a cast o' my office. I shall paint
God in the midst, Madonna and her babe,
Ringed by a bowery flowery angel-brood,
Lilies and vestments and white faces, sweet
As puff on puff of grated orris-root
When ladies crowd to Church at midsummer.
And then i' the front, of course a saint or two—
Saint John, because he saves the Florentines,
Saint Ambrose, who puts down in black and white

The convent's friends and gives them a long day,
And Job, I must have him there past mistake,
The man of Uz (and Us without the z,
Painters who need his patience). Well, all these
Secured at their devotion, up shall come
Out of a corner when you least expect,
As one by a dark stair into a great light,
Music and talking, who but Lippo! I!—
Mazed, motionless and moonstruck—I'm the man!
Back I shrink—what is this I see and hear?
I, caught up with my monk's-things by mistake,
My old serge gown and rope that goes all round,
I, in this presence, this pure company!
Where's a hole, where's a corner for escape?
Then steps a sweet angelic slip of a thing
Forward, puts out a soft palm—"Not so fast!"
—Addresses the celestial presence, "nay—
He made you and devised you, after all,
Though he's none of you! Could Saint John there draw—
His camel-hair make up a painting-brush?
We come to brother Lippo for all that,
Iste perfecit opus!" So, all smile—
I shuffle sideways with my blushing face
Under the cover of a hundred wings
Thrown like a spread of kirtles when you're gay
And play hot cockles, all the doors being shut,
Till, wholly unexpected, in there pops
The hothead husband! Thus I scuttle off
To some safe bench behind, not letting go
The palm of her, the little lily thing
That spoke the good word for me in the nick,
Like the Prior's niece . . . Saint Lucy, I would say.
And so all's saved for me, and for the church
A pretty picture gained. Go, six months hence!

Your hand, sir, and good-bye: no lights, no lights!
The street's hushed, and I know my own way back,
Don't fear me! There's the grey beginning. Zooks!

A Toccata of Galuppi's

I

Oh Galuppi, Baldassaro, this is very sad to find!
I can hardly misconceive you; it would prove me deaf and blind;
But although I take your meaning, 'tis with such a heavy mind!

II

Here you come with your old music, and here's all the good it
      brings.
What, they lived once thus at Venice where the merchants were the
      kings,
Where Saint Mark's is, where the Doges used to wed the sea with
      rings?

III

Ay, because the sea's the street there; and 'tis arched by . . . what
      you call
. . . Shylock's bridge with houses on it, where they kept the
      carnival:
I was never out of England—it's as if I saw it all.

IV

Did young people take their pleasure when the sea was warm in
      May?
Balls and masks begun at midnight, burning ever to midday,
When they made up fresh adventures for the morrow, do you say?

V

Was a lady such a lady, cheeks so round and lips so red,—
On her neck the small face buoyant, like a bell-flower on its bed,

O'er the breast's superb abundance where a man might base his
    head?

VI

Well, and it was graceful of them—they'd break talk off and afford
—She, to bite her mask's black velvet—he, to finger on his sword,
While you sat and played Toccatas, stately at the clavichord?

VII

What? Those lesser thirds so plaintive, sixths diminished, sigh on
    sigh,
Told them something? Those suspensions, those solutions—"Must
    we die?"
Those commiserating sevenths—"Life might last! we can but try!"

VIII

"Were you happy?"—"Yes."—"And are you still as
    happy?"—"Yes. And you?"
—"Then, more kisses!"—"Did *I* stop them, when a million seemed
    so few?"
Hark, the dominant's persistence till it must be answered to!

IX

So, an octave struck the answer. Oh, they praised you, I dare say!
"Brave Galuppi! that was music! good alike at grave and gay!
I can always leave off talking when I hear a master play!"

X

Then they left you for their pleasure: till in due time, one by one,
Some with lives that came to nothing, some with deeds as well
    undone,
Death stepped tacitly and took them where they never see the sun.

But when I sit down to reason, think to take my stand nor swerve,
While I triumph o'er a secret wrung from nature's close reserve,
In you come with your cold music till I creep through every nerve.

XII

Yes, you, like a ghostly cricket, creaking where a house was
    burned:
"Dust and ashes, dead and done with, Venice spent what Venice
    earned.
The soul, doubtless, is immortal—where a soul can be discerned.

XIII

"Yours for instance: you know physics, something of geology,
Mathematics are your pastime; souls shall rise in their degree;
Butterflies may dread extinction,—you'll not die, it cannot be!

XIV

"As for Venice and her people, merely born to bloom and drop,
Here on earth they bore their fruitage, mirth and folly were the
    crop:
What of soul was left, I wonder, when the kissing had to stop?"

XV

"Dust and ashes!" So you creak it, and I want the heart to scold.
Dear dead women, with such hair, too—what's become of all the
    gold
Used to hang and brush their bosoms? I feel chilly and grown old.

By the Fire-Side

I

How well I know what I mean to do
    When the long dark autumn-evenings come,
And where, my soul, is thy pleasant hue?

With the music of all thy voices, dumb
In life's November too!

II

I shall be found by the fire, suppose,
    O'er a great wise book as beseemeth age,
While the shutters flap as the cross-wind blows
    And I turn the page, and I turn the page,
Not verse now, only prose!

III

Till the young ones whisper, finger on lip,
    "There he is at it, deep in Greek:
Now then, or never, out we slip
    To cut from the hazels by the creek
A mainmast for our ship!"

IV

I shall be at it indeed, my friends:
    Greek puts already on either side
Such a branch-work forth as soon extends
    To a vista opening far and wide,
And I pass out where it ends.

V

The outside-frame, like your hazel-trees:
    But the inside-archway widens fast,
And a rarer sort succeeds to these,
    And we slope to Italy at last
And youth, by green degrees.

VI

I follow wherever I am led,
    Knowing so well the leader's hand:
Oh woman-country, wooed not wed,

Loved all the more by earth's male-lands,
Laid to their hearts instead!

VII

Look at the ruined chapel again
   Half-way up in the Alpine gorge!
Is that a tower, I point you plain,
   Or is it a mill, or an iron-forge
Breaks solitude in vain?

VIII

A turn, and we stand in the heart of things;
   The woods are round us, heaped and dim;
From slab to slab how it slips and springs,
   The thread of water single and slim,
Through the ravage some torrent brings!

IX

Does it feed the little lake below?
   That speck of white just on its marge
Is Pella; see, in the evening-glow,
   How sharp the silver spear-heads charge
When Alp meets heaven in snow!

X

On our other side is the straight-up rock;
   And a path is kept 'twixt the gorge and it
By boulder-stones where lichens mock
   The marks on a moth, and small ferns fit
Their teeth to the polished block.

XI

Oh the sense of the yellow mountain-flowers,
   And thorny balls, each three in one,
The chestnuts throw on our path in showers!

For the drop of the woodland fruit's begun,
These early November hours,

XII

That crimson the creeper's leaf across
  Like a splash of blood, intense, abrupt,
O'er a shield else gold from rim to boss,
  And lay it for show on the fairy-cupped
Elf-needled mat of moss,

XIII

By the rose-flesh mushrooms, undivulged
  Last evening—nay, in today's first dew
Yon sudden coral nipple bulged,
  Where a freaked fawn-coloured flaky crew
Of toadstools peep indulged.

XIV

And yonder, at foot of the fronting ridge
  That takes the turn to a range beyond,
Is the chapel reached by the one-arched bridge
  Where the water is stopped in a stagnant pond
Danced over by the midge.

XV

The chapel and bridge are of stone alike,
  Blackish-grey and mostly wet;
Cut hemp-stalks steep in the narrow dike.
  See here again, how the lichens fret
And the roots of the ivy strike!

XVI

Poor little place, where its one priest comes
  On a festa-day, if he comes at all,
To the dozen folk from their scattered homes,

Gathered within that precinct small
By the dozen ways one roams—

XVII

To drop from the charcoal-burners' huts,
    Or climb from the hemp-dressers' low shed,
Leave the grange where the woodman stores his nuts,
    Or the wattled cote where the fowlers spread
Their gear on the rock's bare juts.

XVIII

It has some pretension too, this front,
    With its bit of fresco half-moon-wise
Set over the porch, Art's early wont:
    'Tis John in the Desert, I surmise,
But has borne the weather's brunt—

XIX

Not from the fault of the builder, though,
    For a pent-house properly projects
Where three carved beams make a certain show,
    Dating—good thought of our architect's—
'Five, six, nine, he lets you know.

XX

And all day long a bird sings there,
    And a stray sheep drinks at the pond at times;
The place is silent and aware;
    It has had its scenes, its joys and crimes,
But that is its own affair.

XXI

My perfect wife, my Leonor,
    Oh heart, my own, oh eyes, mine too,
Whom else could I dare look backward for,

With whom beside should I dare pursue
The path grey heads abhor?

XXII

For it leads to a crag's sheer edge with them;
   Youth, flowery all the way, there stops—
Not they; age threatens and they contemn,
   Till they reach the gulf wherein youth drops,
One inch from life's safe hem!

XXIII

With me, youth led . . . I will speak now,
   No longer watch you as you sit
Reading by fire-light, that great brow
   And the spirit-small hand propping it,
Mutely, my heart knows how—

XXIV

When, if I think but deep enough,
   You are wont to answer, prompt as rhyme;
And you, too, find without rebuff
   Response your soul seeks many a time
Piercing its fine flesh-stuff.

XXV

My own, confirm me! If I tread
   This path back, is it not in pride
To think how little I dreamed it led
   To an age so blest that, by its side,
Youth seems the waste instead?

XXVI

My own, see where the years conduct!
   At first, 'twas something our two souls
Should mix as mists do; each is sucked

In each now: on, the new stream rolls,
Whatever rocks obstruct.

XXVII

Think, when our one soul understands
  The great Word which makes all things new,
When earth breaks up and heaven expands,
  How will the change strike me and you
In the house not made with hands?

XXVIII

Oh I must feel your brain prompt mine,
  Your heart anticipate my heart,
You must be just before, in fine,
  See and make me see, for your part,
New depths of the divine!

XXIX

But who could have expected this
  When we two drew together first
Just for the obvious human bliss,
  To satisfy life's daily thirst
With a thing men seldom miss?

XXX

Come back with me to the first of all,
  Let us lean and love it over again,
Let us now forget and now recall,
  Break the rosary in a pearly rain,
And gather what we let fall!

XXXI

What did I say?—that a small bird sings
  All day long, save when a brown pair

Of hawks from the wood float with wide wings
    Strained to a bell: 'gainst noon-day glare
You count the streaks and rings.

XXXII

But at afternoon or almost eve
    'Tis better; then the silence grows
To that degree, you half believe
    It must get rid of what it knows,
Its bosom does so heave.

XXXIII

Hither we walked then, side by side,
    Arm in arm and cheek to cheek,
And still I questioned or replied,
    While my heart, convulsed to really speak,
Lay choking in its pride.

XXXIV

Silent the crumbling bridge we cross,
    And pity and praise the chapel sweet,
And care about the fresco's loss,
    And wish for our souls a like retreat,
And wonder at the moss.

XXXV

Stoop and kneel on the settle under,
    Look through the window's grated square:
Nothing to see! For fear of plunder,
    The cross is down and the altar bare,
As if thieves don't fear thunder.

XXXVI

We stoop and look in through the grate,
    See the little porch and rustic door,
Read duly the dead builder's date;
    Then cross the bridge that we crossed before,
Take the path again—but wait!

XXXVII

Oh moment, one and infinite!
    The water slips o'er stock and stone;
The West is tender, hardly bright:
    How grey at once is the evening grown—
One star, its chrysolite!

XXXVIII

We two stood there with never a third,
    But each by each, as each knew well:
The sights we saw and the sounds we heard,
    The lights and the shades made up a spell
Till the trouble grew and stirred.

XXXIX

Oh, the little more, and how much it is!
    And the little less, and what worlds away!
How a sound shall quicken content to bliss,
    Or a breath suspend the blood's best play,
And life be a proof of this!

XL

Had she willed it, still had stood the screen
    So slight, so sure, 'twixt my love and her:
I could fix her face with a guard between,
    And find her soul as when friends confer,
Friends—lovers that might have been.

XLI

For my heart had a touch of the woodland-time,
    Wanting to sleep now over its best.
Shake the whole tree in the summer-prime,
    But bring to the last leaf no such test!
"Hold the last fast!" runs the rhyme.

XLII

For a chance to make your little much,
    To gain a lover and lose a friend,
Venture the tree and a myriad such,
    When nothing you mar but the year can mend:
But a last leaf—fear to touch!

XLIII

Yet should it unfasten itself and fall
    Eddying down till it find your face
At some slight wind—best chance of all!
    Be your heart henceforth its dwelling-place
You trembled to forestall!

XLIV

Worth how well, those dark grey eyes,
    That hair so dark and dear, how worth
That a man should strive and agonize,
    And taste a veriest hell on earth
For the hope of such a prize!

XLV

You might have turned and tried a man,
    Set him a space to weary and wear,
And prove which suited more your plan,
    His best of hope or his worst despair,
Yet end as he began.

XLVI

But you spared me this, like the heart you are,
  And filled my empty heart at a word.
If two lives join, there is oft a scar,
  They are one and one, with a shadowy third;
One near one is too far.

XLVII

A moment after, and hands unseen
  Were hanging the night around us fast;
But we knew that a bar was broken between
  Life and life: we were mixed at last
In spite of the mortal screen.

XLVIII

The forests had done it; there they stood;
  We caught for a moment the powers at play:
They had mingled us so, for once and good,
  Their work was done—we might go or stay,
They relapsed to their ancient mood.

XLIX

How the world is made for each of us!
  How all we perceive and know in it
Tends to some moment's product thus,
  When a soul declares itself—to wit,
By its fruit, the thing it does!

L

Be hate that fruit or love that fruit,
  It forwards the general deed of man,
And each of the Many helps to recruit
  The life of the race by a general plan;
Each living his own, to boot.

LI

I am named and known by that moment's feat;
  There took my station and degree;
So grew my own small life complete,
  As nature obtained her best of me—
One born to love you, sweet!

LII

And to watch you sink by the fire-side now
  Back again, as you mutely sit
Musing by fire-light, that great brow
  And the spirit-small hand propping it,
Yonder, my heart knows how!

LIII

So, earth has gained by one man the more,
  And the gain of earth must be heaven's gain too;
And the whole is well worth thinking o'er
  When autumn comes: which I mean to do
One day, as I said before.

Any Wife to Any Husband

I

My love, this is the bitterest, that thou—
Who art all truth, and who dost love me now
  As thine eyes say, as thy voice breaks to say—
Shouldst love so truly, and couldst love me still
A whole long life through, had but love its will,
  Would death that leads me from thee brook delay.

II

I have but to be by thee, and thy hand
Will never let mine go, nor heart withstand

The beating of my heart to reach its place.
When shall I look for thee and feel thee gone?
When cry for the old comfort and find none?
    Never, I know! Thy soul is in thy face.

III

Oh, I should fade—'tis willed so! Might I save,
Gladly I would, whatever beauty gave
    Joy to thy sense, for that was precious too.
It is not to be granted. But the soul
Whence the love comes, all ravage leaves that whole;
    Vainly the flesh fades; soul makes all things new.

IV

It would not be because my eye grew dim
Thou couldst not find the love there, thanks to Him
    Who never is dishonoured in the spark
He gave us from his fire of fires, and bade
Remember whence it sprang, nor be afraid
    While that burns on, though all the rest grow dark.

V

So, how thou wouldst be perfect, white and clean
Outside as inside, soul and soul's demesne
    Alike, this body given to show it by!
Oh, three-parts through the worst of life's abyss,
What plaudits from the next world after this,
    Couldst thou repeat a stroke and gain the sky!

VI

And is it not the bitterer to think
That, disengage our hands and thou wilt sink
    Although thy love was love in very deed?
I know that nature! Pass a festive day,

Thou dost not throw its relic-flower away
   Nor bid its music's loitering echo speed.

VII

Thou let'st the stranger's glove lie where it fell;
If old things remain old things all is well,
   For thou art grateful as becomes man best:
And hadst thou only heard me play one tune,
Or viewed me from a window, not so soon
   With thee would such things fade as with the rest.

VIII

I seem to see! We meet and part; 'tis brief;
The book I opened keeps a folded leaf,
   The very chair I sat on, breaks the rank;
That is a portrait of me on the wall—
Three lines, my face comes at so slight a call:
   And for all this, one little hour to thank!

IX

But now, because the hour through years was fixed,
Because our inmost beings met and mixed,
   Because thou once hast loved me—wilt thou dare
Say to thy soul and Who may list beside,
"Therefore she is immortally my bride;
   Chance cannot change my love, nor time impair.

X

"So, what if in the dusk of life that's left,
I, a tired traveller of my sun bereft,
   Look from my path when, mimicking the same,
The fire-fly glimpses past me, come and gone?
—Where was it till the sunset? where anon
   It will be at the sunrise! What's to blame?"

XI

Is it so helpful to thee? Canst thou take
The mimic up, nor, for the true thing's sake,
   Put gently by such efforts at a beam?
Is the remainder of the way so long,
Thou need'st the little solace, thou the strong?
   Watch out thy watch, let weak ones doze and dream!

XII

—Ah, but the fresher faces! "Is it true,"
Thou'lt ask, "some eyes are beautiful and new?
   Some hair,—how can one choose but grasp such wealth?
And if a man would press his lips to lips
Fresh as the wilding hedge-rose-cup there slips
   The dew-drop out of, must it be by stealth?

XIII

"It cannot change the love still kept for Her,
More than if such a picture I prefer
   Passing a day with, to a room's bare side:
The painted form takes nothing she possessed,
Yet, while the Titian's Venus lies at rest,
   A man looks. Once more, what is there to chide?"

XIV

So must I see, from where I sit and watch,
My own self sell myself, my hand attach
   Its warrant to the very thefts from me—
Thy singleness of soul that made me proud.
Thy purity of heart I loved aloud,
   Thy man's-truth I was bold to bid God see!

XV

Love so, then, if thou wilt! Give all thou canst
Away to the new faces—disentranced,

(Say it and think it) obdurate no more:
Re-issue looks and words from the old mint,
Pass them afresh, no matter whose the print
    Image and superscription once they bore!

XVI

Re-coin thyself and give it them to spend,—
It all comes to the same thing at the end,
    Since mine thou wast, mine art and mine shalt be,
Faithful or faithless, sealing up the sum
Or lavish of my treasure, thou must come
    Back to the heart's place here I keep for thee!

XVII

Only, why should it be with stain at all?
Why must I, 'twixt the leaves of coronal,
    Put any kiss of pardon on thy brow?
Why need the other women know so much,
And talk together, "Such the look and such
    The smile he used to love with, then as now!"

XVIII

Might I die last and show thee! Should I find
Such hardship in the few years left behind,
    If free to take and light my lamp, and go
Into thy tomb, and shut the door and sit,
Seeing thy face on those four sides of it
    The better that they are so blank, I know!

XIX

Why, time was what I wanted, to turn o'er
Within my mind each look, get more and more
    By heart each word, too much to learn at first;
And join thee all the fitter for the pause

'Neath the low doorway's lintel. That were cause
    For lingering, though thou called'st, if I durst!

XX

And yet thou art the nobler of us two:
What dare I dream of, that thou canst not do,
    Outstripping my ten small steps with one stride?
I'll say then, here's a trial and a task—
Is it to bear?—if easy, I'll not ask:
    Though love fail, I can trust on in thy pride.

XXI

Pride?—when those eyes forestall the life behind
The death I have to go through!—when I find,
    Now that I want thy help most, all of thee!
What did I fear? Thy love shall hold me fast
Until the little minute's sleep is past
    And I wake saved.—And yet it will not be!

"Childe Roland to the Dark Tower Came"

(SEE EDGAR'S SONG IN *LEAR*)

I

My first thought was, he lied in every word,
    That hoary cripple, with malicious eye
    Askance to watch the working of his lie
On mine, and mouth scarce able to afford
Suppression of the glee, that pursed and scored
    Its edge, at one more victim gained thereby.

II

What else should he be set for, with his staff?
    What, save to waylay with his lies, ensnare

All travellers who might find him posted there,
And ask the road? I guessed what skull-like laugh
Would break, what crutch 'gin write my epitaph
    For pastime in the dusty thoroughfare,

III

If at his counsel I should turn aside
    Into that ominous tract which, all agree,
    Hides the Dark Tower. Yet acquiescingly
I did turn as he pointed: neither pride
Nor hope rekindling at the end descried,
    So much as gladness that some end might be.

IV

For, what with my whole world-wide wandering,
    What with my search drawn out through years, my hope
    Dwindled into a ghost not fit to cope
With that obstreperous joy success would bring,—
I hardly tried now to rebuke the spring
    My heart made, finding failure in its scope.

V

As when a sick man very near to death
    Seems dead indeed, and feels begin and end
    The tears and takes the farewell of each friend,
And hears one bid the other go, draw breath
Freelier outside, ("since all is o'er," he saith,
    "And the blow fallen no grieving can amend");

VI

While some discuss if near the other graves
    Be room enough for this, and when a day
    Suits best for carrying the corpse away,
With care about the banners, scarves and staves:

And still the man hears all, and only craves
    He may not shame such tender love and stay.

VII

Thus, I had so long suffered in this quest,
    Heard failure prophesied so oft, been writ
    So many times among "The Band"—to wit,
The knights who to the Dark Tower's search addressed
Their steps—that just to fail as they, seemed best,
    And all the doubt was now—should I be fit?

VIII

So, quiet as despair, I turned from him,
    That hateful cripple, out of his highway
    Into the path he pointed. All the day
Had been a dreary one at best, and dim
Was settling to its close, yet shot one grim
    Red leer to see the plain catch its estray.

IX

For mark! no sooner was I fairly found
    Pledged to the plain, after a pace or two,
    Than, pausing to throw backward a last view
O'er the safe road, 'twas gone; grey plain all round:
Nothing but plain to the horizon's bound.
    I might go on; naught else remained to do.

X

So, on I went. I think I never saw
    Such starved ignoble nature; nothing throve:
    For flowers—as well expect a cedar grove!
But cockle, spurge, according to their law
Might propagate their kind, with none to awe,
    You'd think; a burr had been a treasure-trove.

XI

No! penury, inertness and grimace,
   In some strange sort, were the land's portion. "See
   Or shut your eyes," said Nature peevishly,
"It nothing skills: I cannot help my case:
'Tis the Last Judgement's fire must cure this place,
   Calcine its clods and set my prisoners free."

XII

If there pushed any ragged thistle-stalk
   Above its mates, the head was chopped; the bents
   Were jealous else. What made those holes and rents
In the dock's harsh swarth leaves, bruised as to balk
All hope of greenness? 'tis a brute must walk
   Pashing their life out, with a brute's intents.

XIII

As for the grass, it grew as scant as hair
   In leprosy; thin dry blades pricked the mud
   Which underneath looked kneaded up with blood.
One stiff blind horse, his every bone a-stare,
Stood stupefied, however he came there:
   Thrust out past service from the devil's stud!

XIV

Alive? he might be dead for aught I know,
   With that red gaunt and colloped neck a-strain,
   And shut eyes underneath the rusty mane;
Seldom went such grotesqueness with such woe;
I never saw a brute I hated so;
   He must be wicked to deserve such pain.

XV

I shut my eyes and turned them on my heart.
  As a man calls for wine before he fights,
  I asked one draught of earlier, happier sights,
Ere fitly I could hope to play my part.
Think first, fight afterwards—the soldier's art:
  One taste of the old time sets all to rights.

XVI

Not it! I fancied Cuthbert's reddening face
  Beneath its garniture of curly gold,
  Dear fellow, till I almost felt him fold
An arm in mine to fix me to the place,
That way he used. Alas, one night's disgrace!
  Out went my heart's new fire and left it cold.

XVII

Giles then, the soul of honour—there he stands
  Frank as ten years ago when knighted first.
  What honest man should dare (he said) he durst.
Good—but the scene shifts—faugh! what hangman-hands
Pin to his breast a parchment? His own bands
  Read it. Poor traitor, spit upon and curst!

XVIII

Better this present than a past like that;
  Back therefore to my darkening path again!
  No sound, no sight as far as eye could strain.
Will the night send a howlet or a bat?
I asked: when something on the dismal flat
  Came to arrest my thoughts and change their train.

XIX

A sudden little river crossed my path
  As unexpected as a serpent comes.

No sluggish tide congenial to the glooms;
This, as it frothed by, might have been a bath
For the fiend's glowing hoof—to see the wrath
   Of its black eddy bespate with flakes and spumes.

XX

So petty yet so spiteful! All along,
   Low scrubby alders kneeled down over it;
   Drenched willows flung them headlong in a fit
Of mute despair, a suicidal throng:
The river which had done them all the wrong,
   Whate'er that was, rolled by, deterred no whit.

XXI

Which, while I forded,—good saints, how I feared
   To set my foot upon a dead man's cheek,
   Each step, or feel the spear I thrust to seek
For hollows, tangled in his hair or beard!
—It may have been a water-rat I speared,
   But, ugh! it sounded like a baby's shriek.

XXII

Glad was I when I reached the other bank.
   Now for a better country. Vain presage!
   Who were the strugglers, what war did they wage,
Whose savage trample thus could pad the dank
Soil to a plash? Toads in a poisoned tank,
   Or wild cats in a red-hot iron cage—

XXIII

The fight must so have seemed in that fell cirque.
   What penned them there, with all the plain to choose?
   No foot-print leading to that horrid mews,
None out of it. Mad brewage set to work

Their brains, no doubt, like galley-slaves the Turk
   Pits for his pastime, Christians against Jews.

XXIV

And more than that—a furlong on—why, there!
   What bad use was that engine for, that wheel,
   Or brake, not wheel—that harrow fit to reel
Men's bodies out like silk? with all the air
Of Tophet's tool, on earth left unaware,
   Or brought to sharpen its rusty teeth of steel.

XXV

Then came a bit of stubbed ground, once a wood,
   Next a marsh, it would seem, and now mere earth
   Desperate and done with; (so a fool finds mirth,
Makes a thing and then mars it, till his mood
Changes and off he goes!) within a rood—
   Bog, clay and rubble, sand and stark black dearth.

XXVI

Now blotches rankling, coloured gay and grim,
   Now patches where some leanness of the soil's
   Broke into moss or substances like boils;
Then came some palsied oak, a cleft in him
Like a distorted mouth that splits its rim
   Gaping at death, and dies while it recoils.

XXVII

And just as far as ever from the end!
   Naught in the distance but the evening, naught
   To point my footstep further! At the thought,
A great black bird, Apollyon's bosom-friend,
Sailed past, nor beat his wide wing dragon-penned
   That brushed my cap—perchance the guide I sought.

XXVIII

For, looking up, aware I somehow grew,
   'Spite of the dusk, the plain had given place
    All round to mountains—with such name to grace
Mere ugly heights and heaps now stolen in view.
How thus they had surprised me,—solve it, you!
   How to get from them was no clearer case.

XXIX

Yet half I seemed to recognize some trick
   Of mischief happened to me, God knows when—
    In a bad dream perhaps. Here ended, then,
Progress this way. When, in the very nick
Of giving up, one time more, came a click
   As when a trap shuts—you're inside the den!

XXX

Burningly it came on me all at once,
   This was the place! those two hills on the right,
    Crouched like two bulls locked horn in horn in fight;
While to the left, a tall scalped mountain . . . Dunce,
Dotard, a-dozing at the very nonce,
   After a life spent training for the sight!

XXXI

What in the midst lay but the Tower itself?
   The round squat turret, blind as the fool's heart,
    Built of brown stone, without a counterpart
In the whole world. The tempest's mocking elf
Points to the shipman thus the unseen shelf
   He strikes on, only when the timbers start.

XXXII

Not see? because of night perhaps?—why, day
    Came back again for that! before it left,
    The dying sunset kindled through a cleft:
The hills, like giants at a hunting, lay,
Chin upon hand, to see the game at bay,—
    "Now stab and end the creature—to the heft!"

XXXIII

Not hear? when noise was everywhere! it tolled
    Increasing like a bell. Names in my ears
    Of all the lost adventurers my peers,—
How such a one was strong, and such was bold,
And such was fortunate, yet each of old
    Lost, lost! one moment knelled the woe of years.

XXXIV

There they stood, ranged along the hill-sides, met
    To view the last of me, a living frame
    For one more picture! in a sheet of flame
I saw them and I knew them all. And yet
Dauntless the slug-horn to my lips I set,
    And blew. *"Childe Roland to the Dark Tower came."*

The Statue and the Bust

There's a palace in Florence, the world knows well,
And a statue watches it from the square,
And this story of both do our townsmen tell.

Ages ago, a lady there,
At the farthest window facing the East
Asked, "Who rides by with the royal air?"

The bridesmaids' prattle around her ceased;
She leaned forth, one on either hand;
They saw how the blush of the bride increased—

They felt by its beats her heart expand—
As one at each ear and both in a breath
Whispered, "The Great-Duke Ferdinand."

That self-same instant, underneath,
The Duke rode past in his idle way,
Empty and fine like a swordless sheath.

Gay he rode, with a friend as gay,
Till he threw his head back—"Who is she?"
—"A bride the Riccardi brings home today."

Hair in heaps lay heavily
Over a pale brow spirit-pure—
Carved like the heart of the coal-black tree,

Crisped like a war-steed's encolure—
And vainly sought to dissemble her eyes
Of the blackest black our eyes endure.

And lo, a blade for a knight's emprise
Filled the fine empty sheath of a man,—
The Duke grew straightway brave and wise.

He looked at her, as a lover can;
She looked at him, as one who awakes:
The past was a sleep, and her life began.

Now, love so ordered for both their sakes,
A feast was held that selfsame night
In the pile which the mighty shadow makes.

(For Via Larga is three-parts light,
But the palace overshadows one,
Because of a crime which may God requite!

To Florence and God the wrong was done,
Through the first republic's murder there
By Cosimo and his cursèd son.)

The Duke (with the statue's face in the square)
Turned in the midst of his multitude
At the bright approach of the bridal pair.

Face to face the lovers stood
A single minute and no more,
While the bridegroom bent as a man subdued—

Bowed till his bonnet brushed the floor—
For the Duke on the lady a kiss conferred,
As the courtly custom was of yore.

In a minute can lovers exchange a word?
If a word did pass, which I do not think,
Only one out of the thousand heard.

That was the bridegroom. At day's brink
He and his bride were alone at last
In a bedchamber by a taper's blink.

Calmly he said that her lot was cast,
That the door she had passed was shut on her
Till the final catafalque repassed.

The world meanwhile, its noise and stir,
Through a certain window facing the East,
She could watch like a convent's chronicler.

Since passing the door might lead to a feast,
And a feast might lead to so much beside,
He, of many evils, chose the least.

"Freely I choose too," said the bride—
"Your window and its world suffice,"
Replied the tongue, while the heart replied—

"If I spend the night with that devil twice,
May his window serve as my loop of hell
Whence a damned soul looks on paradise!

"I fly to the Duke who loves me well,
Sit by his side and laugh at sorrow
Ere I count another ave-bell.

" 'Tis only the coat of a page to borrow,
And tie my hair in a horse-boy's trim,
And I save my soul—but not tomorrow"—

(She checked herself and her eye grew dim)
"My father tarries to bless my state:
I must keep it one day more for him.

"Is one day more so long to wait?
Moreover the Duke rides past, I know;
We shall see each other, sure as fate."

She turned on her side and slept. Just so!
So we resolve on a thing and sleep:
So did the lady, ages ago.

That night the Duke said, "Dear or cheap
As the cost of this cup of bliss may prove
To body or soul, I will drain it deep."

And on the morrow, bold with love,
He beckoned the bridegroom (close on call,
As his duty bade, by the Duke's alcove)

And smiled " 'Twas a very funeral,
Your lady will think, this feast of ours,—
A shame to efface, whate'er befall!

"What if we break from the Arno bowers,
And try if Petraja, cool and green,
Cure last night's fault with this morning's flowers?"

The bridegroom, not a thought to be seen
On his steady brow and quiet mouth,
Said, "Too much favour for me so mean!

"But, alas! my lady leaves the South;
Each wind that comes from the Apennine
Is a menace to her tender youth:

"Nor a way exists, the wise opine,
If she quits her palace twice this year,
To avert the flower of life's decline."

Quoth the Duke, "A sage and a kindly fear.
Moreover Petraja is cold this spring:
Be our feast tonight as usual here!"

And then to himself—"Which night shall bring
Thy bride to her lover's embraces, fool—
Or I am the fool, and thou art the king!

"Yet my passion must wait a night, nor cool—
For tonight the Envoy arrives from France
Whose heart I unlock with thyself, my tool.

"I need thee still and might miss perchance.
Today is not wholly lost, beside,
With its hope of my lady's countenance:

"For I ride—what should I do but ride?
And passing her palace, if I list,
May glance at its window—well betide!"

So said, so done: nor the lady missed
One ray that broke from the ardent brow,
Nor a curl of the lips where the spirit kissed.

Be sure that each renewed the vow,
No morrow's sun should arise and set
And leave them then as it left them now.

But next day passed, and next day yet,
With still fresh cause to wait one day more
Ere each leaped over the parapet.

And still, as love's brief morning wore,
With a gentle start, half smile, half sigh,
They found love not as it seemed before.

They thought it would work infallibly,
But not in despite of heaven and earth:
The rose would blow when the storm passed by.

Meantime they could profit in winter's dearth
By store of fruits that supplant the rose:
The world and its ways have a certain worth:

And to press a point while these oppose
Were simple policy; better wait:
We lose no friends and we gain no foes.

Meantime, worse fates than a lover's fate,
Who daily may ride and pass and look
Where his lady watches behind the grate!

And she—she watched the square like a book
Holding one picture and only one,
Which daily to find she undertook:

When the picture was reached the book was done,
And she turned from the picture at night to scheme
Of tearing it out for herself next sun.

So weeks grew months, years; gleam by gleam
The glory dropped from their youth and love,
And both perceived they had dreamed a dream;

Which hovered as dreams do, still above:
But who can take a dream for a truth?
Oh, hide our eyes from the next remove!

One day as the lady saw her youth
Depart, and the silver thread that streaked
Her hair, and, worn by the serpent's tooth,

The brow so puckered, the chin so peaked,—
And wondered who the woman was,
Hollow-eyed and haggard-cheeked,

Fronting her silent in the glass—
"Summon here," she suddenly said,
"Before the rest of my old self pass,

"Him, the Carver, a hand to aid,
Who fashions the clay no love will change,
And fixes a beauty never to fade.

"Let Robbia's craft so apt and strange
Arrest the remains of young and fair,
And rivet them while the seasons range.

"Make me a face on the window there,
Waiting as ever, mute the while,
My love to pass below in the square!

"And let me think that it may beguile
Dreary days which the dead must spend
Down in their darkness under the aisle,

"To say, 'What matters it at the end?
I did no more while my heart was warm
Than does that image, my pale-faced friend.'

"Where is the use of the lip's red charm,
The heaven of hair, the pride of the brow,
And the blood that blues the inside arm—

"Unless we turn, as the soul knows how,
The earthly gift to an end divine?
A lady of clay is as good, I trow."

But long ere Robbia's cornice, fine,
With flowers and fruits which leaves enlace,
Was set where now is the empty shrine—

(And, leaning out of a bright blue space,
As a ghost might lean from a chink of sky,
The passionate pale lady's face—

Eyeing ever, with earnest eye
And quick-turned neck at its breathless stretch,
Some one who ever is passing by—)

The Duke had sighed like the simplest wretch
In Florence, "Youth—my dream escapes!
Will its record stay?" And he bade them fetch

Some subtle moulder of brazen shapes—
"Can the soul, the will, die out of a man
Ere his body find the grave that gapes?

"John of Douay shall effect my plan,
Set me on horseback here aloft,
Alive, as the crafty sculptor can,

"In the very square I have crossed so oft:
That men may admire, when future suns
Shall touch the eyes to a purpose soft,

"While the mouth and the brow stay brave in bronze—
Admire and say, 'When he was alive
How he would take his pleasure once!'

"And it shall go hard but I contrive
To listen the while, and laugh in my tomb
At idleness which aspires to strive."

◆ ◆

So! While these wait the trump of doom,
How do their spirits pass, I wonder,
Nights and days in the narrow room?

Still, I suppose, they sit and ponder
What a gift life was, ages ago,
Six steps out of the chapel yonder.

Only they see not God, I know,
Nor all that chivalry of his,
The soldier-saints who, row on row,

Burn upward each to his point of bliss—
Since, the end of life being manifest,
He had burned his way through the world to this.

I hear you reproach, "But delay was best,
For their end was a crime."—Oh, a crime will do
As well, I reply, to serve for a test,

As a virtue golden through and through,
Sufficient to vindicate itself
And prove its worth at a moment's view!

Must a game be played for the sake of pelf?
Where a button goes, 'twere an epigram
To offer the stamp of the very Guelph.

The true has no value beyond the sham:
As well the counter as coin, I submit,
When your table's a hat, and your prize a dram.

Stake your counter as boldly every whit,
Venture as warily, use the same skill,
Do your best, whether winning or losing it,

If you choose to play!—is my principle.
Let a man contend to the uttermost
For his life's set prize, be it what it will!

The counter our lovers staked was lost
As surely as if it were lawful coin:
And the sin I impute to each frustrate ghost

Is—the unlit lamp and the ungirt loin,
Though the end in sight was a vice, I say.
You of the virtue (we issue join)
How strive you? *De te, fabula.*

Love in a Life

I

Room after room,
I hunt the house through
We inhabit together.
Heart, fear nothing, for, heart, thou shalt find her—
Next time, herself!—not the trouble behind her
Left in the curtain, the couch's perfume!
As she brushed it, the cornice-wreath blossomed anew:
Yon looking-glass gleamed at the wave of her feather.

II

Yet the day wears,
And door succeeds door;
I try the fresh fortune—
Range the wide house from the wing to the centre.
Still the same chance! she goes out as I enter.
Spend my whole day in the quest,—who cares?
But 'tis twilight, you see,—with such suites to explore,
Such closets to search, such alcoves to importune!

How It Strikes a Contemporary

I only knew one poet in my life:
And this, or something like it, was his way.

  You saw go up and down Valladolid,
A man of mark, to know next time you saw.
His very serviceable suit of black
Was courtly once and conscientious still,
And many might have worn it, though none did:
The cloak, that somewhat shone and showed the threads,
Had purpose, and the ruff, significance.
He walked and tapped the pavement with his cane,
Scenting the world, looking it full in face,
An old dog, bald and blindish, at his heels.
They turned up, now, the alley by the church,
That leads nowhither; now, they breathed themselves
On the main promenade just at the wrong time:
You'd come upon his scrutinizing hat,
Making a peaked shade blacker than itself
Against the single window spared some house
Intact yet with its mouldered Moorish work,—
Or else surprise the ferrel of his stick
Trying the mortar's temper 'tween the chinks
Of some new shop a-building, French and fine.
He stood and watched the cobbler at his trade,
The man who slices lemons into drink,
The coffee-roaster's brazier, and the boys
That volunteer to help him turn its winch.
He glanced o'er books on stalls with half an eye,
And fly-leaf ballads on the vendor's string,
And broad-edge bold-print posters by the wall.
He took such cognizance of men and things,
If any beat a horse, you felt he saw;

If any cursed a woman, he took note;
Yet stared at nobody,—you stared at him,
And found, less to your pleasure than surprise,
He seemed to know you and expect as much.
So, next time that a neighbour's tongue was loosed,
It marked the shameful and notorious fact,
We had among us, not so much a spy,
As a recording chief-inquisitor,
The town's true master if the town but knew!
We merely kept a governor for form,
While this man walked about and took account
Of all thought, said and acted, then went home,
And wrote it fully to our Lord the King
Who has an itch to know things, he knows why,
And reads them in his bedroom of a night.
Oh, you might smile! there wanted not a touch,
A tang of . . . well, it was not wholly ease
As back into your mind the man's look came.
Stricken in years a little,—such a brow
His eyes had to live under!—clear as flint
On either side the formidable nose
Curved, cut and coloured like an eagle's claw.
Had he to do with A.'s surprising fate?
When altogether old B. disappeared
And young C. got his mistress,—was't our friend,
His letter to the King, that did it all?
What paid the bloodless man for so much pains?
Our Lord the King has favourites manifold,
And shifts his ministry some once a month;
Our city gets new governors at whiles,—
But never word or sign, that I could hear,
Notified to this man about the streets
The King's approval of those letters conned
The last thing duly at the dead of night.
Did the man love his office? Frowned our Lord,

Exhorting when none heard—"Beseech me not!
Too far above my people,—beneath me!
I set the watch,—how should the people know?
Forget them, keep me all the more in mind!"
Was some such understanding 'twixt the two?

I found no truth in one report at least—
That if you tracked him to his home, down lanes
Beyond the Jewry, and as clean to pace,
You found he ate his supper in a room
Blazing with lights, four Titians on the wall,
And twenty naked girls to change his plate!
Poor man, he lived another kind of life
In that new stuccoed third house by the bridge,
Fresh-painted, rather smart than otherwise!
The whole street might o'erlook him as he sat,
Leg crossing leg, one foot on the dog's back,
Playing a decent cribbage with his maid
(Jacynth, you're sure her name was) o'er the cheese
And fruit, three red halves of starved winter-pears,
Or treat of radishes in April. Nine,
Ten, struck the church clock, straight to bed went he.

My father, like the man of sense he was,
Would point him out to me a dozen times;
" 'St—'St," he'd whisper, "the Corregidor!"
I had been used to think that personage
Was one with lacquered breeches, lustrous belt,
And feathers like a forest in his hat,
Who blew a trumpet and proclaimed the news,
Announced the bull-fights, gave each church its turn,
And memorized the miracle in vogue!
He had a great observance from us boys;
We were in error; that was not the man.

I'd like now, yet had haply been afraid,
To have just looked, when this man came to die,
And seen who lined the clean gay garret-sides
And stood about the neat low truckle-bed,
With the heavenly manner of relieving guard.
Here had been, mark, the general-in-chief,
Through a whole campaign of the world's life and death,
Doing the King's work all the dim day long,
In his old coat and up to knees in mud,
Smoked like a herring, dining on a crust,—
And, now the day was won, relieved at once!
No further show or need for that old coat,
You are sure, for one thing! Bless us, all the while
How sprucely we are dressed out, you and I!
A second, and the angels alter that.
Well, I could never write a verse,—could you?
Let's to the Prado and make the most of time.

Memorabilia

I

Ah, did you once see Shelley plain,
   And did he stop and speak to you
And did you speak to him again?
   How strange it seems and new!

II

But you were living before that,
   And also you are living after;
And the memory I started at—
   My starting moves your laughter.

III

I crossed a moor, with a name of its own
   And a certain use in the world no doubt,

Yet a hand's-breadth of it shines alone
'Mid the blank miles round about:

IV

For there I picked up on the heather
And there I put inside my breast
A moulted feather, an eagle-feather!
Well, I forget the rest.

Andrea del Sarto

(CALLED "THE FAULTLESS PAINTER")

But do not let us quarrel any more,
No, my Lucrezia; bear with me for once:
Sit down and all shall happen as you wish.
You turn your face, but does it bring your heart?
I'll work then for your friend's friend, never fear,
Treat his own subject after his own way,
Fix his own time, accept too his own price,
And shut the money into this small hand
When next it takes mine. Will it? tenderly?
Oh, I'll content him,—but tomorrow, Love!
I often am much wearier than you think,
This evening more than usual, and it seems
As if—forgive now—should you let me sit
Here by the window with your hand in mine
And look a half-hour forth on Fiesole,
Both of one mind, as married people use,
Quietly, quietly the evening through,
I might get up tomorrow to my work
Cheerful and fresh as ever. Let us try.
Tomorrow, how you shall be glad for this!
Your soft hand is a woman of itself,
And mine the man's bared breast she curls inside.

Don't count the time lost, neither; you must serve
For each of the five pictures we require:
It saves a model. So! keep looking so—
My serpentining beauty, rounds on rounds!
—How could you ever prick those perfect ears,
Even to put the pearl there! oh, so sweet—
My face, my moon, my everybody's moon,
Which everybody looks on and calls his,
And, I suppose, is looked on by in turn,
While she looks—no one's: very dear, no less.
You smile? why, there's my picture ready made,
There's what we painters call our harmony!
A common greyness silvers everything,—
All in a twilight, you and I alike
—You, at the point of your first pride in me
(That's gone you know),—but I, at every point;
My youth, my hope, my art, being all toned down
To yonder sober pleasant Fiesole.
There's the bell clinking from the chapel-top;
That length of convent-wall across the way
Holds the trees safer, huddled more inside;
The last monk leaves the garden; days decrease,
And autumn grows, autumn in everything.
Eh? the whole seems to fall into a shape
As if I saw alike my work and self
And all that I was born to be and do,
A twilight-piece. Love, we are in God's hand.
How strange now, looks the life he makes us lead;
So free we seem, so fettered fast we are!
I feel he laid the fetter: let it lie!
This chamber for example—turn your head—
All that's behind us! You don't understand
Nor care to understand about my art,
But you can hear at least when people speak:

And that cartoon, the second from the door
—It is the thing, Love! so such things should be—
Behold Madonna!—I am bold to say.
I can do with my pencil what I know,
What I see, what at bottom of my heart
I wish for, if I ever wish so deep—
Do easily, too—when I say, perfectly,
I do not boast, perhaps: yourself are judge,
Who listened to the Legate's talk last week,
And just as much they used to say in France.
At any rate 'tis easy, all of it!
No sketches first, no studies, that's long past:
I do what many dream of, all their lives,
—Dream? strive to do, and agonize to do,
And fail in doing. I could count twenty such
On twice your fingers, and not leave this town,
Who strive—you don't know how the others strive
To paint a little thing like that you smeared
Carelessly passing with your robes afloat,—
Yet do much less, so much less, Someone says,
(I know his name, no matter)—so much less!
Well, less is more, Lucrezia: I am judged.
There burns a truer light of God in them,
In their vexed beating stuffed and stopped-up brain,
Heart, or whate'er else, than goes on to prompt
This low-pulsed forthright craftsman's hand of mine.
Their works drop groundward, but themselves, I know,
Reach many a time a heaven that's shut to me,
Enter and take their place there sure enough,
Though they come back and cannot tell the world.
My works are nearer heaven, but I sit here.
The sudden blood of these men! at a word—
Praise them, it boils, or blame them, it boils too.
I, painting from myself and to myself,

Know what I do, am unmoved by men's blame
Or their praise either. Somebody remarks
Morello's outline there is wrongly traced,
His hue mistaken; what of that? or else,
Rightly traced and well ordered; what of that?
Speak as they please, what does the mountain care?
Ah, but a man's reach should exceed his grasp,
Or what's a heaven for? All is silver-grey
Placid and perfect with my art: the worse!
I know both what I want and what might gain,
And yet how profitless to know, to sigh
"Had I been two, another and myself,
Our head would have o'erlooked the world!" No doubt.
Yonder's a work now, of that famous youth
The Urbinate who died five years ago.
('Tis copied, George Vasari sent it me.)
Well, I can fancy how he did it all,
Pouring his soul, with kings and popes to see,
Reaching, that heaven might so replenish him,
Above and through his art—for it gives way;
That arm is wrongly put—and there again—
A fault to pardon in the drawing's lines,
Its body, so to speak: its soul is right,
He means right—that, a child may understand.
Still, what an arm! and I could alter it:
But all the play, the insight and the stretch—
Out of me, out of me! And wherefore out?
Had you enjoined them on me, given me soul,
We might have risen to Rafael, I and you!
Nay, Love, you did give all I asked, I think—
More than I merit, yes, by many times.
But had you—oh, with the same perfect brow,
And perfect eyes, and more than perfect mouth,
And the low voice my soul hears, as a bird

The fowler's pipe, and follows to the snare—
Had you, with these the same, but brought a mind!
Some women do so. Had the mouth there urged
"God and the glory! never care for gain.
The present by the future, what is that?
Live for fame, side by side with Agnolo!
Rafael is waiting: up to God, all three!"
I might have done it for you. So it seems:
Perhaps not. All is as God over-rules.
Beside, incentives come from the soul's self;
The rest avail not. Why do I need you?
What wife had Rafael, or has Agnolo?
In this world, who can do a thing, will not;
And who would do it, cannot, I perceive:
Yet the will's somewhat—somewhat, too, the power—
And thus we half-men struggle. At the end,
God, I conclude, compensates, punishes.
'Tis safer for me, if the award be strict,
That I am something underrated here,
Poor this long while, despised, to speak the truth.
I dared not, do you know, leave home all day,
For fear of chancing on the Paris lords.
The best is when they pass and look aside;
But they speak sometimes; I must bear it all.
Well may they speak! That Francis, that first time,
And that long festal year at Fontainebleau!
I surely then could sometimes leave the ground,
Put on the glory, Rafael's daily wear,
In that humane great monarch's golden look,—
One finger in his beard or twisted curl
Over his mouth's good mark that made the smile,
One arm about my shoulder, round my neck,
The jingle of his gold chain in my ear,
I painting proudly with his breath on me,

All his court round him, seeing with his eyes,
Such frank French eyes, and such a fire of souls
Profuse, my hand kept plying by those hearts,—
And, best of all, this, this, this face beyond,
This in the background, waiting on my work,
To crown the issue with a last reward!
A good time, was it not, my kingly days?
And had you not grown restless . . . but I know—
'Tis done and past; 'twas right, my instinct said;
Too live the life grew, golden and not grey,
And I'm the weak-eyed bat no sun should tempt
Out of the grange whose four walls make his world.
How could it end in any other way?
You called me, and I came home to your heart.
The triumph was—to reach and stay there; since
I reached it ere the triumph, what is lost?
Let my hands frame your face in your hair's gold,
You beautiful Lucrezia that are mine!
"Rafael did this, Andrea painted that;
The Roman's is the better when you pray,
But still the other's Virgin was his wife—"
Men will excuse me. I am glad to judge
Both pictures in your presence; clearer grows
My better fortune, I resolve to think.
For, do you know, Lucrezia, as God lives,
Said one day Agnolo, his very self,
To Rafael . . . I have known it all these years . . .
(When the young man was flaming out his thoughts
Upon a palace-wall for Rome to see,
Too lifted up in heart because of it)
"Friend, there's a certain sorry little scrub
Goes up and down our Florence, none cares how,
Who, were he set to plan and execute
As you are, pricked on by your popes and kings,

Would bring the sweat into that brow of yours!"
To Rafael's!—And indeed the arm is wrong.
I hardly dare . . . yet, only you to see,
Give the chalk here—quick, thus the line should go!
Ay, but the soul! he's Rafael! rub it out!
Still, all I care for, if he spoke the truth,
(What he? why, who but Michel Agnolo?
Do you forget already words like those?)
If really there was such a chance, so lost,—
Is, whether you're—not grateful—but more pleased.
Well, let me think so. And you smile indeed!
This hour has been an hour! Another smile?
If you would sit thus by me every night
I should work better, do you comprehend?
I mean that I should earn more, give you more.
See, it is settled dusk now; there's a star;
Morello's gone, the watch-lights show the wall,
The cue-owls speak the name we call them by.
Come from the window, love,—come in, at last,
Inside the melancholy little house
We built to be so gay with. God is just.
King Francis may forgive me: oft at nights
When I look up from painting, eyes tired out,
The walls become illumined, brick from brick
Distinct, instead of mortar, fierce bright gold,
That gold of his I did cement them with!
Let us but love each other. Must you go?
That Cousin here again? he waits outside?
Must see you—you, and not with me? Those loans?
More gaming debts to pay? you smiled for that?
Well, let smiles buy me! have you more to spend?
While hand and eye and something of a heart
Are left me, work's my ware, and what's it worth?
I'll pay my fancy. Only let me sit

The grey remainder of the evening out,
Idle, you call it, and muse perfectly
How I could paint, were I but back in France,
One picture, just one more—the Virgin's face,
Not yours this time! I want you at my side
To hear them—that is, Michel Agnolo—
Judge all I do and tell you of its worth.
Will you? Tomorrow, satisfy your friend.
I take the subjects for his corridor,
Finish the portrait out of hand—there, there,
And throw him in another thing or two
If he demurs; the whole should prove enough
To pay for this same Cousin's freak. Beside,
What's better and what's all I care about,
Get you the thirteen scudi for the ruff!
Love, does that please you? Ah, but what does he,
The Cousin! what does he to please you more?

    I am grown peaceful as old age tonight.
I regret little, I would change still less.
Since there my past life lies, why alter it?
The very wrong to Francis!—it is true
I took his coin, was tempted and complied,
And built this house and sinned, and all is said.
My father and my mother died of want.
Well, had I riches of my own? you see
How one gets rich! Let each one bear his lot.
They were born poor, lived poor, and poor they died:
And I have laboured somewhat in my time
And not been paid profusely. Some good son
Paint my two hundred pictures—let him try!
No doubt, there's something strikes a balance. Yes,
You loved me quite enough, it seems tonight.
This must suffice me here. What would one have?
In heaven, perhaps, new chances, one more chance—

Four great walls in the New Jerusalem,
Meted on each side by the angel's reed,
For Leonard, Rafael, Agnolo and me
To cover—the three first without a wife,
While I have mine! So—still they overcome
Because there's still Lucrezia,—as I choose.

Again the Cousin's whistle! Go, my Love.

Women and Roses

I

I dream of a red-rose tree.
And which of its roses three
Is the dearest rose to me?

II

Round and round, like a dance of snow
In a dazzling drift, as its guardians, go
Floating the women faded for ages,
Sculptured in stone, on the poet's pages.
Then follow women fresh and gay,
Living and loving and loved today.
Last, in the rear, flee the multitude of maidens,
Beauties yet unborn. And all, to one cadence,
They circle their rose on my rose tree.

III

Dear rose, thy term is reached,
Thy leaf hangs loose and bleached:
Bees pass it unimpeached.

IV

Stay then, stoop, since I cannot climb,
You, great shapes of the antique time!

How shall I fix you, fire you, freeze you,
Break my heart at your feet to please you?
Oh, to possess and be possessed!
Hearts that beat 'neath each pallid breast!
Once but of love, the poesy, the passion,
Drink but once and die!—In vain, the same fashion,
They circle their rose on my rose tree.

V

Dear rose, thy joy's undimmed,
Thy cup is ruby-rimmed,
Thy cup's heart nectar-brimmed.

VI

Deep, as drops from a statue's plinth
The bee sucked in by the hyacinth,
So will I bury me while burning,
Quench like him at a plunge my yearning,
Eyes in your eyes, lips on your lips!
Fold me fast where the cincture slips,
Prison all my soul in eternities of pleasure,
Girdle me for once! But no—the old measure,
They circle their rose on my rose tree.

VII

Dear rose without a thorn,
Thy bud's the babe unborn:
First streak of a new morn.

VIII

Wings, lend wings for the cold, the clear!
What is far conquers what is near.
Roses will bloom nor want beholders,
Sprung from the dust where our flesh moulders.

What shall arrive with the cycle's change?
A novel grace and a beauty strange.
I will make an Eve, be the artist that began her,
Shaped her to his mind!—Alas! in like manner
They circle their rose on my rose tree.

Protus

Among these latter busts we count by scores,
Half-emperors and quarter-emperors,
Each with his bay-leaf fillet, loose-thonged vest,
Loric and low-browed Gorgon on the breast,—
One loves a baby face, with violets there,
Violets instead of laurel in the hair,
As those were all the little locks could bear.

Now read here. "Protus ends a period
Of empery beginning with a god;
Born in the porphyry chamber at Byzant,
Queens by his cradle, proud and ministrant:
And if he quickened breath there, 'twould like fire
Pantingly through the dim vast realm transpire.
A fame that he was missing spread afar:
The world, from its four corners, rose in war,
Till he was borne out on a balcony
To pacify the world when it should see.
The captains ranged before him, one, his hand
Made baby points at, gained the chief command.
And day by day more beautiful he grew
In shape, all said, in feature and in hue,
While young Greek sculptors, gazing on the child,
Became with old Greek sculpture reconciled.
Already sages laboured to condense
In easy tomes a life's experience:

And artists took grave counsel to impart
In one breath and one hand-sweep, all their art—
To make his graces prompt as blossoming
Of plentifully-watered palms in spring:
Since well beseems it, whoso mounts the throne,
For beauty, knowledge, strength, should stand alone,
And mortals love the letters of his name."

—Stop! Have you turned two pages? Still the same.
New reign, same date. The scribe goes on to say
How that same year, on such a month and day,
"John the Pannonian, groundedly believed
A blacksmith's bastard, whose hard hand reprieved
The Empire from its fate the year before,—
Came, had a mind to take the crown, and wore
The same for six years (during which the Huns
Kept off their fingers from us), till his sons
Put something in his liquor"—and so forth.
Then a new reign. Stay—"Take at its just worth"
(Subjoins an annotator) "what I give
As hearsay. Some think, John let Protus live
And slip away. 'Tis said, he reached man's age
At some blind northern court; made, first a page,
Then tutor to the children; last, of use
About the hunting-stables. I deduce
He wrote the little tract 'On worming dogs,'
Whereof the name in sundry catalogues
Is extant yet. A Protus of the race
Is rumoured to have died a monk in Thrace,—
And if the same, he reached senility."

Here's John the Smith's rough-hammered head. Great eye,
Gross jaw and griped lips do what granite can
To give you the crown-grasper. What a man!

Cleon

"As certain also of your own poets have said"—

Cleon the poet (from the sprinkled isles,
Lily on lily, that o'erlace the sea,
And laugh their pride when the light wave lisps "Greece")—
To Protus in his Tyranny: much health!

    They give thy letter to me, even now:
I read and seem as if I heard thee speak.
The master of thy galley still unlades
Gift after gift; they block my court at last
And pile themselves along its portico
Royal with sunset, like a thought of thee:
And one white she-slave from the group dispersed
Of black and white slaves (like the chequer-work
Pavement, at once my nation's work and gift,
Now covered with this settle-down of doves),
One lyric woman, in her crocus vest
Woven of sea-wools, with her two white hands
Commends to me the strainer and the cup
Thy lip hath bettered ere it blesses mine.

    Well-counselled, king, in thy munificence!
For so shall men remark, in such an act
Of love for him whose song gives life its joy,
Thy recognition of the use of life;
Nor call thy spirit barely adequate
To help on life in straight ways, broad enough
For vulgar souls, by ruling and the rest.
Thou, in the daily building of thy tower,—
Whether in fierce and sudden spasms of toil,
Or through dim lulls of unapparent growth,

Or when the general work 'mid good acclaim
Climbed with the eye to cheer the architect,—
Didst ne'er engage in work for mere work's sake—
Had'st ever in thy heart the luring hope
Of some eventual rest a-top of it,
Whence, all the tumult of the building hushed,
Thou first of men mightst look out to the East:
The vulgar saw thy tower, thou sawest the sun.
For this, I promise on thy festival
To pour libation, looking o'er the sea,
Making this slave narrate thy fortunes, speak
Thy great words, and describe thy royal face—
Wishing thee wholly where Zeus lives the most,
Within the eventual element of calm.

Thy letter's first requirement meets me here.
It is as thou hast heard: in one short life
I, Cleon, have effected all those things
Thou wonderingly dost enumerate.
That epos on thy hundred plates of gold
Is mine,—and also mine the little chant,
So sure to rise from every fishing-bark
When, lights at prow, the seamen haul their net.
The image of the sun-god on the phare,
Men turn from the sun's self to see, is mine;
The Poecile, o'er-storied its whole length,
As thou didst hear, with painting, is mine too.
I know the true proportions of a man
And woman also, not observed before;
And I have written three books on the soul,
Proving absurd all written hitherto,
And putting us to ignorance again.
For music,—why, I have combined the moods,
Inventing one. In brief, all arts are mine;

Thus much the people know and recognize,
Throughout our seventeen islands. Marvel not.
We of these latter days, with greater mind
Than our forerunners, since more composite,
Look not so great, beside their simple way,
To a judge who only sees one way at once,
One mind-point and no other at a time,—
Compares the small part of a man of us
With some whole man of the heroic age,
Great in his way—not ours, nor meant for ours.
And ours is greater, had we skill to know:
For, what we call this life of men on earth,
This sequence of the soul's achievements here
Being, as I find much reason to conceive,
Intended to be viewed eventually
As a great whole, not analysed to parts,
But each part having reference to all,—
How shall a certain part, pronounced complete,
Endure effacement by another part?
Was the thing done?—then, what's to do again?
See, in the chequered pavement opposite,
Suppose the artist made a perfect rhomb,
And next a lozenge, then a trapezoid—
He did not overlay them, superimpose
The new upon the old and blot it out,
But laid them on a level in his work,
Making at last a picture; there it lies.
So, first the perfect separate forms were made,
The portions of mankind; and after, so,
Occurred the combination of the same.
For where had been a progress, otherwise?
Mankind, made up of all the single men,—
In such a synthesis the labour ends.
Now mark me! those divine men of old time

Have reached, thou sayest well, each at one point
The outside verge that rounds our faculty;
And where they reached, who can do more than reach?
It takes but little water just to touch
At some one point the inside of a sphere,
And, as we turn the sphere, touch all the rest
In due succession: but the finer air
Which not so palpably nor obviously,
Though no less universally, can touch
The whole circumference of that emptied sphere,
Fills it more fully than the water did;
Holds thrice the weight of water in itself
Resolved into a subtler element.
And yet the vulgar call the sphere first full
Up to the visible height—and after, void;
Not knowing air's more hidden properties.
And thus our soul, misknown, cries out to Zeus
To vindicate his purpose in our life:
Why stay we on the earth unless to grow?
Long since, I imaged, wrote the fiction out,
That he or other god descended here
And, once for all, showed simultaneously
What, in its nature, never can be shown,
Piecemeal or in succession;—showed, I say,
The worth both absolute and relative
Of all his children from the birth of time,
His instruments for all appointed work.
I now go on to image,—might we hear
The judgement which should give the due to each,
Show where the labour lay and where the ease,
And prove Zeus' self, the latent everywhere!
This is a dream:—but no dream, let us hope,
That years and days, the summers and the springs,
Follow each other with unwaning powers.

The grapes which dye thy wine are richer far,
Through culture, than the wild wealth of the rock;
The suave plum than the savage-tasted drupe;
The pastured honey-bee drops choicer sweet;
The flowers turn double, and the leaves turn flowers;
That young and tender crescent-moon, thy slave,
Sleeping above her robe as buoyed by clouds,
Refines upon the women of my youth.
What, and the soul alone deteriorates?
I have not chanted verse like Homer, no—
Nor swept string like Terpander, no—nor carved
And painted men like Phidias and his friend:
I am not great as they are, point by point.
But I have entered into sympathy
With these four, running these into one soul,
Who, separate, ignored each other's art.
Say, is it nothing that I know them all?
The wild flower was the larger; I have dashed
Rose-blood upon its petals, pricked its cup's
Honey with wine, and driven its seed to fruit,
And show a better flower if not so large:
I stand myself. Refer this to the gods
Whose gift alone it is! which, shall I dare
(All pride apart) upon the absurd pretext
That such a gift by chance lay in my hand,
Discourse of lightly or depreciate?
It might have fallen to another's hand: what then?
I pass too surely: let at least truth stay!

    And next, of what thou followest on to ask.
This being with me as I declare, O king,
My works, in all these varicoloured kinds,
So done by me, accepted so by men—
Thou askest, if (my soul thus in men's hearts)

I must not be accounted to attain
The very crown and proper end of life?
Inquiring thence how, now life closeth up,
I face death with success in my right hand:
Whether I fear death less than dost thyself
The fortunate of men? "For" (writest thou)
"Thou leavest much behind, while I leave naught.
Thy life stays in the poems men shall sing,
The pictures men shall study; while my life,
Complete and whole now in its power and joy,
Dies altogether with my brain and arm,
Is lost indeed; since, what survives myself?
The brazen statue to o'erlook my grave,
Set on the promontory which I named.
And that—some supple courtier of my heir
Shall use its robed and sceptred arm, perhaps,
To fix the rope to, which best drags it down.
I go then: triumph thou, who dost not go!"

Nay, thou art worthy of hearing my whole mind.
Is this apparent, when thou turn'st to muse
Upon the scheme of earth and man in chief,
That admiration grows as knowledge grows?
That imperfection means perfection hid,
Reserved in part, to grace the after-time?
If, in the morning of philosophy,
Ere aught had been recorded, nay perceived,
Thou, with the light now in thee, couldst have looked
On all earth's tenantry, from worm to bird,
Ere man, her last, appeared upon the stage—
Thou wouldst have seen them perfect, and deduced
The perfectness of others yet unseen.
Conceding which,—had Zeus then questioned thee
"Shall I go on a step, improve on this,

Do more for visible creatures than is done?"
Thou wouldst have answered, "Ay, by making each
Grow conscious in himself—by that alone.
All's perfect else: the shell sucks fast the rock,
The fish strikes through the sea, the snake both swims
And slides, forth range the beasts, the birds take flight,
Till life's mechanics can no further go—
And all this joy in natural life is put
Like fire from off thy finger into each,
So exquisitely perfect is the same.
But 'tis pure fire, and they mere matter are;
It has them, not they it: and so I choose
For man, thy last premeditated work
(If I might add a glory to the scheme)
That a third thing should stand apart from both,
A quality arise within his soul,
Which, intro-active, made to supervise
And feel the force it has, may view itself,
And so be happy." Man might live at first
The animal life: but is there nothing more?
In due time, let him critically learn
How he lives; and, the more he gets to know
Of his own life's adaptabilities,
The more joy-giving will his life become.
Thus man, who hath this quality, is best.

But thou, king, hadst more reasonably said:
"Let progress end at once,—man make no step
Beyond the natural man, the better beast,
Using his senses, not the sense of sense."
In man there's failure, only since he left
The lower and inconscious forms of life.
We called it an advance, the rendering plain
Man's spirit might grow conscious of man's life,

And, by new lore so added to the old,
Take each step higher over the brute's head.
This grew the only life, the pleasure-house,
Watch-tower and treasure-fortress of the soul,
Which whole surrounding flats of natural life
Seemed only fit to yield subsistence to;
A tower that crowns a country. But alas,
The soul now climbs it just to perish there!
For thence we have discovered ('tis no dream—
We know this, which we had not else perceived)
That there's a world of capability
For joy, spread round about us, meant for us,
Inviting us; and still the soul craves all,
And still the flesh replies, "Take no jot more
Than ere thou clombst the tower to look abroad!
Nay, so much less as that fatigue has brought
Deduction to it." We struggle, fain to enlarge
Our bounded physical recipiency,
Increase our power, supply fresh oil to life,
Repair the waste of age and sickness: no,
It skills not! life's inadequate to joy,
As the soul sees joy, tempting life to take.
They praise a fountain in my garden here
Wherein a Naiad sends the water-bow
Thin from her tube; she smiles to see it rise.
What if I told her, it is just a thread
From that great river which the hills shut up,
And mock her with my leave to take the same?
The artificer has given her one small tube
Past power to widen or exchange—what boots
To know she might spout oceans if she could?
She cannot lift beyond her first thin thread:
And so a man can use but a man's joy
While he sees God's. Is it for Zeus to boast,

"See, man, how happy I live, and despair—
That I may be still happier—for thy use!"
If this were so, we could not thank our lord,
As hearts beat on to doing; 'tis not so—
Malice it is not. Is it carelessness?
Still, no. If care—where is the sign? I ask,
And get no answer, and agree in sum,
O king, with thy profound discouragement,
Who seest the wider but to sigh the more.
Most progress is most failure: thou sayest well.

The last point now:—thou dost except a case—
Holding joy not impossible to one
With artist-gifts—to such a man as I
Who leave behind me living works indeed;
For, such a poem, such a painting lives.
What? dost thou verily trip upon a word,
Confound the accurate view of what joy is
(Caught somewhat clearer by my eyes than thine)
With feeling joy? confound the knowing how
And showing how to live (my faculty)
With actually living?—Otherwise
Where is the artist's vantage o'er the king?
Because in my great epos I display
How divers men young, strong, fair, wise, can act—
Is this as though I acted? if I paint,
Carve the young Phoebus, am I therefore young?
Methinks I'm older that I bowed myself
The many years of pain that taught me art!
Indeed, to know is something, and to prove
How all this beauty might be enjoyed, is more:
But, knowing naught, to enjoy is something too.
Yon rower, with the moulded muscles there,
Lowering the sail, is nearer it than I.

I can write love-odes: thy fair slave's an ode.
I get to sing of love, when grown too grey
For being beloved: she turns to that young man,
The muscles all a-ripple on his back.
I know the joy of kingship: well, thou art king!

"But," sayest thou—(and I marvel, I repeat
To find thee trip on such a mere word) "what
Thou writest, paintest, stays; that does not die:
Sappho survives, because we sing her songs,
And Aeschylus, because we read his plays!"
Why, if they live still, let them come and take
Thy slave in my despite, drink from thy cup,
Speak in my place. Thou diest while I survive?
Say rather that my fate is deadlier still,
In this, that every day my sense of joy
Grows more acute, my soul (intensified
By power and insight) more enlarged, more keen;
While every day my hairs fall more and more,
My hand shakes, and the heavy years increase—
The horror quickening still from year to year,
The consummation coming past escape
When I shall know most, and yet least enjoy—
When all my works wherein I prove my worth,
Being present still to mock me in men's mouths,
Alive still, in the praise of such as thou,
I, I the feeling, thinking, acting man,
The man who loved his life so over-much,
Sleep in my urn. It is so horrible,
I dare at times imagine to my need
Some future state revealed to us by Zeus,
Unlimited in capability
For joy, as this is in desire for joy,
—To seek which, the joy-hunger forces us:
That, stung by straitness of our life, made strait

On purpose to make prized the life at large—
Freed by the throbbing impulse we call death,
We burst there as the worm into the fly,
Who, while a worm still, wants his wings. But no!
Zeus has not yet revealed it; and alas,
He must have done so, were it possible!

Live long and happy, and in that thought die:
Glad for what was! Farewell. And for the rest,
I cannot tell thy messenger aright
Where to deliver what he bears of thine
To one called Paulus; we have heard his fame
Indeed, if Christus be not one with him—
I know not, nor am troubled much to know.
Thou canst not think a mere barbarian Jew,
As Paulus proves to be, one circumcised,
Hath access to a secret shut from us?
Thou wrongest our philosophy, O king,
In stooping to inquire of such an one,
As if his answer could impose at all!
He writeth, doth he? well, and he may write.
Oh, the Jew findeth scholars! certain slaves
Who touched on this same isle, preached him and Christ;
And (as I gathered from a bystander)
Their doctrine could be held by no sane man.

Two in the Campagna

I

I wonder do you feel today
    As I have felt since, hand in hand,
We sat down on the grass, to stray
    In spirit better through the land,
This morn of Rome and May?

II

For me, I touched a thought, I know,
    Has tantalized me many times,
(Like turns of thread the spiders throw
    Mocking across our path) for rhymes
To catch at and let go.

III

Help me to hold it! First it left
    The yellowing fennel, run to seed
There, branching from the brickwork's cleft,
    Some old tomb's ruin: yonder weed
Took up the floating weft,

IV

Where one small orange cup amassed
    Five beetles,—blind and green they grope
Among the honey-meal: and last,
    Everywhere on the grassy slope
I traced it. Hold it fast!

V

The champaign with its endless fleece
    Of feathery grasses everywhere!
Silence and passion, joy and peace,
    An everlasting wash of air—
Rome's ghost since her decease.

VI

Such life here, through such lengths of hours,
    Such miracles performed in play,
Such primal naked forms of flowers,
    Such letting nature have her way
While heaven looks from its towers!

VII

How say you? Let us, O my dove,
  Let us be unashamed of soul,
As earth lies bare to heaven above!
  How is it under our control
To love or not to love?

VIII

I would that you were all to me,
  You that are just so much, no more.
Nor yours nor mine, nor slave nor free!
  Where does the fault lie? What the core
O' the wound, since wound must be?

IX

I would I could adopt your will,
  See with your eyes, and set my heart
Beating by yours, and drink my fill
  At your soul's springs,—your part my part
In life, for good and ill.

X

No. I yearn upward, touch you close,
  Then stand away. I kiss your cheek,
Catch your soul's warmth,—I pluck the rose
  And love it more than tongue can speak—
Then the good minute goes.

XI

Already how am I so far
  Out of that minute? Must I go
Still like the thistle-ball, no bar,
  Onward, whenever light winds blow,
Fixed by no friendly star?

XII

Just when I seemed about to learn!
    Where is the thread now? Off again!
The old trick! Only I discern—
    Infinite passion, and the pain
Of finite hearts that yearn.

A Grammarian's Funeral

SHORTLY AFTER THE REVIVAL OF LEARNING IN EUROPE

Let us begin and carry up this corpse,
    Singing together.
Leave we the common crofts, the vulgar thorpes
    Each in its tether
Sleeping safe on the bosom of the plain,
    Cared-for till cock-crow:
Look out if yonder be not day again
    Rimming the rock-row!
That's the appropriate country; there, man's thought,
    Rarer, intenser,
Self-gathered for an outbreak, as it ought,
    Chafes in the censer.
Leave we the unlettered plain its herd and crop;
    Seek we sepulture
On a tall mountain, citied to the top,
    Crowded with culture!
All the peaks soar, but one the rest excels;
    Clouds overcome it;
No! yonder sparkle is the citadel's
    Circling its summit.
Thither our path lies; wind we up the heights;
    Wait ye the warning?
Our low life was the level's and the night's;
    He's for the morning.

Step to a tune, square chests, erect each head,
  'Ware the beholders!
This is our master, famous calm and dead,
  Borne on our shoulders.

Sleep, crop and herd! sleep, darkling thorpe and croft,
  Safe from the weather!
He, whom we convoy to his grave aloft,
  Singing together,
He was a man born with thy face and throat,
  Lyric Apollo!
Long he lived nameless: how should spring take note
  Winter would follow?
Till lo, the little touch, and youth was gone!
  Cramped and diminished,
Moaned he, "New measures, other feet anon!
  My dance is finished?"
No, that's the world's way: (keep the mountain-side,
  Make for the city!)
He knew the signal, and stepped on with pride
  Over men's pity;
Left play for work, and grappled with the world
  Bent on escaping:
"What's in the scroll," quoth he, "thou keepest furled?
  Show me their shaping,
Theirs who most studied man, the bard and sage,—
  Give!"—So, he gowned him,
Straight got by heart that book to its last page:
  Learned, we found him.
Yea, but we found him bald too, eyes like lead,
  Accents uncertain:
"Time to taste life," another would have said,
  "Up with the curtain!"
This man said rather, "Actual life comes next?
  Patience a moment!

Grant I have mastered learning's crabbed text,
    Still there's the comment.
Let me know all! Prate not of most or least,
    Painful or easy!
Even to the crumbs I'd fain eat up the feast,
    Ay, nor feel queasy."
Oh, such a life as he resolved to live,
    When he had learned it,
When he had gathered all books had to give!
    Sooner, he spurned it.
Image the whole, then execute the parts—
    Fancy the fabric
Quite, ere you build, ere steel strike fire from quartz,
    Ere mortar dab brick!

(Here's the town-gate reached: there's the market-place
    Gaping before us.)
Yea, this in him was the peculiar grace
    (Hearten our chorus!)
That before living he'd learn how to live—
    No end to learning:
Earn the means first—God surely will contrive
    Use for our earning.
Others mistrust and say, "But time escapes:
    Live now or never!"
He said, "What's time? Leave Now for dogs and apes!
    Man has Forever."
Back to his book then: deeper drooped his head:
    Calculus racked him:
Leaden before, his eyes grew dross of lead:
    Tussis attacked him.
"Now, master, take a little rest!"—not he!
    (Caution redoubled,
Step two abreast, the way winds narrowly!)
    Not a whit troubled

Back to his studies, fresher than at first,
    Fierce as a dragon
He (soul-hydroptic with a sacred thirst)
    Sucked at the flagon.
Oh, if we draw a circle premature,
    Heedless of far gain,
Greedy for quick returns of profit, sure
    Bad is our bargain!
Was it not great? did not he throw on God,
    (He loves the burthen)—
God's task to make the heavenly period
    Perfect the earthen?
Did not he magnify the mind, show clear
    Just what it all meant?
He would not discount life, as fools do here,
    Paid by instalment.
He ventured neck or nothing—heaven's success
    Found, or earth's failure:
"Wilt thou trust death or not?" He answered "Yes:
    Hence with life's pale lure!"
That low man seeks a little thing to do,
    Sees it and does it:
This high man, with a great thing to pursue,
    Dies ere he knows it.
That low man goes on adding one to one,
    His hundred's soon hit:
This high man, aiming at a million,
    Misses an unit.
That, has the world here—should he need the next,
    Let the world mind him!
This, throws himself on God, and unperplexed
    Seeking shall find him.
So, with the throttling hands of death at strife,
    Ground he at grammar;
Still, through the rattle, parts of speech were rife:

While he could stammer
He settled *Hoti*'s business—let it be!—
    Properly based *Oun*—
Gave us the doctrine of the enclitic *De,*
    Dead from the waist down.
Well, here's the platform, here's the proper place:
    Hail to your purlieus,
All ye highfliers of the feathered race,
    Swallows and curlews!
Here's the top-peak; the multitude below
    Live, for they can, there:
This man decided not to Live but Know—
    Bury this man there?
Here—here's his place, where meteors shoot, clouds form,
    Lightnings are loosened,
Stars come and go! Let joy break with the storm,
    Peace let the dew send!
Lofty designs must close in like effects:
    Loftily lying,
Leave him—still loftier than the world suspects,
    Living and dying.

"Transcendentalism: A Poem in Twelve Books"

Stop playing, poet! May a brother speak?
'Tis you speak, that's your error. Song's our art:
Whereas you please to speak these naked thoughts
Instead of draping them in sights and sounds.
—True thoughts, good thoughts, thoughts fit to treasure up!
But why such long prolusion and display,
Such turning and adjustment of the harp,
And taking it upon your breast, at length,
Only to speak dry words across its strings?
Stark-naked thought is in request enough:

Speak prose and hollo it till Europe hears!
The six-foot Swiss tube, braced about with bark,
Which helps the hunter's voice from Alp to Alp—
Exchange our harp for that,—who hinders you?

But here's your fault; grown men want thought, you think;
Thought's what they mean by verse, and seek in verse.
Boys seek for images and melody,
Men must have reason—so, you aim at men.
Quite otherwise! Objects throng our youth, 'tis true;
We see and hear and do not wonder much:
If you could tell us what they mean, indeed!
As German Boehme never cared for plants
Until it happed, a-walking in the fields,
He noticed all at once that plants could speak,
Nay, turned with loosened tongue to talk with him.
That day the daisy had an eye indeed—
Colloquized with the cowslip on such themes!
We find them extant yet in Jacob's prose.
But by the time youth slips a stage or two
While reading prose in that tough book he wrote
(Collating and emendating the same
And settling on the sense most to our mind),
We shut the clasps and find life's summer past.
Then, who helps more, pray, to repair our loss—
Another Boehme with a tougher book
And subtler meanings of what roses say,—
Or some stout Mage like him of Halberstadt,
John, who made things Boehme wrote thoughts about?
He with a "look you!" vents a brace of rhymes,
And in there breaks the sudden rose herself,
Over us, under, round us every side,
Nay, in and out the tables and the chairs
And musty volumes, Boehme's book and all,—

Buries us with a glory, young once more,
Pouring heaven into this shut house of life.

So come, the harp back to your heart again!
You are a poem, though your poem's naught.
The best of all you showed before, believe,
Was your own boy-face o'er the finer chords
Bent, following the cherub at the top
That points to God with his paired half-moon wings.

One Word More

TO E.B.B.

1855

I

There they are, my fifty men and women
Naming me the fifty poems finished!
Take them, Love, the book and me together:
Where the heart lies, let the brain lie also.

II

Rafael made a century of sonnets,
Made and wrote them in a certain volume
Dinted with the silver-pointed pencil
Else he only used to draw Madonnas:
These, the world might view—but one, the volume.
Who that one, you ask? Your heart instructs you.
Did she live and love it all her life-time?
Did she drop, his lady of the sonnets,
Die, and let it drop beside her pillow
Where it lay in place of Rafael's glory,
Rafael's cheek so duteous and so loving—
Cheek, the world was wont to hail a painter's,
Rafael's cheek, her love had turned a poet's?

III

You and I would rather read that volume,
(Taken to his beating bosom by it)
Lean and list the bosom-beats of Rafael,
Would we not? than wonder at Madonnas—
Her, San Sisto names, and Her, Foligno,
Her, that visits Florence in a vision,
Her, that's left with lilies in the Louvre—
Seen by us and all the world in circle.

IV

You and I will never read that volume.
Guido Reni, like his own eye's apple
Guarded long the treasure-book and loved it.
Guido Reni dying, all Bologna
Cried, and the world cried too, "Ours, the treasure!"
Suddenly, as rare things will, it vanished.

V

Dante once prepared to paint an angel:
Whom to please? You whisper "Beatrice."
While he mused and traced it and retraced it,
(Peradventure with a pen corroded
Still by drops of that hot ink he dipped for,
When, his left-hand i' the hair o' the wicked,
Back he held the brow and pricked its stigma,
Bit into the live man's flesh for parchment,
Loosed him, laughed to see the writing rankle,
Let the wretch go festering through Florence)—
Dante, who loved well because he hated,
Hated wickedness that hinders loving,
Dante standing, studying his angel,—
In there broke the folk of his Inferno.
Says he—"Certain people of importance"
(Such he gave his daily dreadful line to)

"Entered and would seize, forsooth, the poet."
Says the poet—"Then I stopped my painting."

VI

You and I would rather see that angel,
Painted by the tenderness of Dante,
Would we not?—than read a fresh Inferno.

VII

You and I will never see that picture.
While he mused on love and Beatrice,
While he softened o'er his outlined angel,
In they broke, those "people of importance":
We and Bice bear the loss for ever.

VIII

What of Rafael's sonnets, Dante's picture?
This: no artist lives and loves, that longs not
Once, and only once, and for one only,
(Ah, the prize!) to find his love a language
Fit and fair and simple and sufficient—
Using nature that's an art to others,
Not, this one time, art that's turned his nature.
Ay, of all the artists living, loving,
None but would forego his proper dowry,—
Does he paint? he fain would write a poem,—
Does he write? he fain would paint a picture,
Put to proof art alien to the artist's,
Once, and only once, and for one only,
So to be the man and leave the artist,
Gain the man's joy, miss the artist's sorrow.

IX

Wherefore? Heaven's gift takes earth's abatement!
He who smites the rock and spreads the water,
Bidding drink and live a crowd beneath him,
Even he, the minute makes immortal,
Proves, perchance, but mortal in the minute,
Desecrates, belike, the deed in doing.
While he smites, how can he but remember,
So he smote before, in such a peril,
When they stood and mocked—"Shall smiting help us?"
When they drank and sneered—"A stroke is easy!"
When they wiped their mouths and went their journey,
Throwing him for thanks—"But drought was pleasant."
Thus old memories mar the actual triumph;
Thus the doing savours of disrelish;
Thus achievement lacks a gracious somewhat;
O'er-importuned brows becloud the mandate,
Carelessness or consciousness—the gesture.
For he bears an ancient wrong about him,
Sees and knows again those phalanxed faces,
Hears, yet one time more, the 'customed prelude—
"How shouldst thou, of all men, smite, and save us?"
Guesses what is like to prove the sequel—
"Egypt's flesh-pots—nay, the drought was better."

X

Oh, the crowd must have emphatic warrant!
Theirs, the Sinai-forehead's cloven brilliance,
Right-arm's rod-sweep, tongue's imperial fiat.
Never dares the man put off the prophet.

XI

Did he love one face from out the thousands,
(Were she Jethro's daughter, white and wifely,

Were she but the Aethiopian bondslave,)
He would envy yon dumb patient camel,
Keeping a reserve of scanty water
Meant to save his own life in the desert;
Ready in the desert to deliver
(Kneeling down to let his breast be opened)
Hoard and life together for his mistress.

XII

I shall never, in the years remaining,
Paint you pictures, no, nor carve you statues,
Make you music that should all-express me;
So it seems: I stand on my attainment.
This of verse alone, one life allows me;
Verse and nothing else have I to give you.
Other heights in other lives, God willing:
All the gifts from all the heights, your own, Love!

XIII

Yet a semblance of resource avails us—
Shade so finely touched, love's sense must seize it.
Take these lines, look lovingly and nearly,
Lines I write the first time and the last time.
He who works in fresco, steals a hair-brush,
Curbs the liberal hand, subservient proudly,
Cramps his spirit, crowds its all in little,
Makes a strange art of an art familiar,
Fills his lady's missal-marge with flowerets.
He who blows through bronze, may breathe through silver,
Fitly serenade a slumbrous princess.
He who writes, may write for once as I do.

XIV

Love, you saw me gather men and women,
Live or dead or fashioned by my fancy,

Enter each and all, and use their service,
Speak from every mouth,—the speech, a poem.
Hardly shall I tell my joys and sorrows,
Hopes and fears, belief and disbelieving:
I am mine and yours—the rest be all men's,
Karshish, Cleon, Norbert and the fifty.
Let me speak this once in my true person,
Not as Lippo, Roland or Andrea,
Though the fruit of speech be just this sentence:
Pray you, look on these my men and women,
Take and keep my fifty poems finished;
Where my heart lies, let my brain lie also!
Poor the speech; be how I speak, for all things.

XV

Not but that you know me! Lo, the moon's self!
Here in London, yonder late in Florence,
Still we find her face, the thrice-transfigured.
Curving on a sky imbrued with colour,
Drifted over Fiesole by twilight,
Came she, our new crescent of a hair's-breadth.
Full she flared it, lamping Samminiato,
Rounder 'twixt the cypresses and rounder,
Perfect till the nightingales applauded.
Now, a piece of her old self, impoverished,
Hard to greet, she traverses the houseroofs,
Hurries with unhandsome thrift of silver,
Goes dispiritedly, glad to finish.

XVI

What, there's nothing in the moon noteworthy?
Nay: for if that moon could love a mortal,
Use, to charm him (so to fit a fancy),
All her magic ('tis the old sweet mythos)
She would turn a new side to her mortal,

Side unseen of herdsman, huntsman, steersman—
Blank to Zoroaster on his terrace,
Blind to Galileo on his turret,
Dumb to Homer, dumb to Keats—him, even!
Think, the wonder of the moonstruck mortal—
When she turns round, comes again in heaven,
Opens out anew for worse or better!
Proves she like some portent of an iceberg
Swimming full upon the ship it founders,
Hungry with huge teeth of splintered crystals?
Proves she as the paved work of a sapphire
Seen by Moses when he climbed the mountain?
Moses, Aaron, Nadab and Abihu
Climbed and saw the very God, the Highest,
Stand upon the paved work of a sapphire.
Like the bodied heaven in his clearness
Shone the stone, the sapphire of that paved work,
When they ate and drank and saw God also!

XVII

What were seen? None knows, none ever shall know.
Only this is sure—the sight were other,
Not the moon's same side, born late in Florence,
Dying now impoverished here in London.
God be thanked, the meanest of his creatures
Boasts two soul-sides, one to face the world with,
One to show a woman when he loves her!

XVIII

This I say of me, but think of you, Love!
This to you—yourself my moon of poets!
Ah, but that's the world's side, there's the wonder,
Thus they see you, praise you, think they know you!
There, in turn I stand with them and praise you—

Out of my own self, I dare to phrase it.
But the best is when I glide from out them,
Cross a step or two of dubious twilight,
Come out on the other side, the novel
Silent silver lights and darks undreamed of,
Where I hush and bless myself with silence.

XIX

Oh, their Rafael of the dear Madonnas,
Oh, their Dante of the dread Inferno,
Wrote one song—and in my brain I sing it,
Drew one angel—borne, see, on my bosom!

R.B.

FROM *DRAMATIS PERSONAE,* 1864

James Lee's Wife

I. JAMES LEE'S WIFE SPEAKS AT THE WINDOW

I

Ah, Love, but a day
   And the world has changed!
The sun's away,
   And the bird estranged;
The wind has dropped,
   And the sky's deranged:
Summer has stopped.

II

Look in my eyes!
   Wilt thou change too?
Should I fear surprise?

Shall I find aught new
In the old and dear,
  In the good and true,
With the changing year?

III

Thou art a man,
  But I am thy love.
For the lake, its swan;
  For the dell, its dove;
And for thee— (oh, haste!)
  Me, to bend above,
Me, to hold embraced.

II. BY THE FIRESIDE

I

Is all our fire of shipwreck wood,
  Oak and pine?
Oh, for the ills half-understood,
  The dim dead woe
  Long ago
Befallen this bitter coast of France!
Well, poor sailors took their chance;
  I take mine.

II

A ruddy shaft our fire must shoot
  O'er the sea:
Do sailors eye the casement—mute,
  Drenched and stark,
  From their bark—
And envy, gnash their teeth for hate

O' the warm safe house and happy freight
   —Thee and me?

III

God help you, sailors, at your need!
   Spare the curse!
For some ships, safe in port indeed,
   Rot and rust,
   Run to dust,
All through worms i' the wood, which crept,
Gnawed our hearts out while we slept:
   That is worse.

IV

Who lived here before us two?
   Old-world pairs.
Did a woman ever—would I knew!—
   Watch the man
   With whom began
Love's voyage full-sail,—(now, gnash your teeth!)
When planks start, open hell beneath
   Unawares?

III. IN THE DOORWAY

I

The swallow has set her six young on the rail,
   And looks sea-ward:
The water's in stripes like a snake, olive-pale
   To the leeward,—
On the weather-side, black, spotted white with the wind.
"Good fortune departs, and disaster's behind,"—
Hark, the wind with its wants and its infinite wail!

II

Our fig-tree, that leaned for the saltness, has furled
    Her five fingers,
Each leaf like a hand opened wide to the world
    Where there lingers
No glint of the gold, Summer sent for her sake:
How the vines writhe in rows, each impaled on its stake!
My heart shrivels up and my spirit shrinks curled.

III

Yet here are we two; we have love, house enough,
    With the field there,
This house of four rooms, that field red and rough,
    Though it yield there,
For the rabbit that robs, scarce a blade or a bent;
If a magpie alight now, it seems an event;
And they both will be gone at November's rebuff.

IV

But why must cold spread? but wherefore bring change
    To the spirit,
God meant should mate his with an infinite range,
    And inherit
His power to put life in the darkness and cold?
Oh, live and love worthily, bear and be bold!
Whom Summer made friends of, let Winter estrange!

IV. ALONG THE BEACH

I

I will be quiet and talk with you,
    And reason why you are wrong.
You wanted my love—is that much true?

And so I did love, so I do:
　　What has come of it all along?

II

I took you—how could I otherwise?
　　For a world to me, and more;
For all, love greatens and glorifies
Till God's a-glow, to the loving eyes,
　　In what was mere earth before.

III

Yes, earth—yes, mere ignoble earth!
　　Now do I mis-state, mistake?
Do I wrong your weakness and call it worth?
Expect all harvest, dread no dearth,
　　Seal my sense up for your sake?

IV

Oh, Love, Love, no, Love! not so, indeed!
　　You were just weak earth, I knew:
With much in you waste, with many a weed,
And plenty of passions run to seed,
　　But a little good grain too.

V

And such as you were, I took you for mine:
　　Did not you find me yours,
To watch the olive and wait the vine,
And wonder when rivers of oil and wine
　　Would flow, as the Book assures?

VI

Well, and if none of these good things came,
　　What did the failure prove?

The man was my whole world, all the same,
With his flowers to praise or his weeds to blame,
    And, either or both, to love.

VII

Yet this turns now to a fault—there! there!
    That I do love, watch too long,
And wait too well, and weary and wear;
And 'tis all an old story, and my despair
    Fit subject for some new song:

VIII

"How the light, light love, he has wings to fly
    At suspicion of a bond:
My wisdom has bidden your pleasure good-bye,
Which will turn up next in a laughing eye,
    And why should you look beyond?"

V. ON THE CLIFF

I

I leaned on the turf,
I looked at a rock
Left dry by the surf;
For the turf, to call it grass were to mock:
Dead to the roots, so deep was done
The work of the summer sun.

II

And the rock lay flat
As an anvil's face:
No iron like that!
Baked dry; of a weed, of a shell, no trace:

Sunshine outside, but ice at the core,
Death's altar by the lone shore.

III

On the turf, sprang gay
With his films of blue,
No cricket, I'll say,
But a warhorse, barded and chanfroned too,
The gift of a quixote-mage to his knight,
Real fairy, with wings all right.

IV

On the rock, they scorch
Like a drop of fire
From a brandished torch,
Fall two red fans of a butterfly:
No turf, no rock: in their ugly stead,
See, wonderful blue and red!

V

Is it not so
With the minds of men?
The level and low,
The burnt and bare, in themselves; but then
With such a blue and red grace, not theirs,—
Love settling unawares!

VI. READING A BOOK, UNDER THE CLIFF

I

"Still ailing, Wind? Wilt be appeased or no?
    Which needs the other's office, thou or I?
Dost want to be disburthened of a woe,

And can, in truth, my voice untie
Its links, and let it go?

II

"Art thou a dumb wronged thing that would be righted,
    Entrusting thus thy cause to me? Forbear!
No tongue can mend such pleadings; faith, requited
    With falsehood,—love, at last aware
Of scorn,—hopes, early blighted,—

III

"We have them; but I know not any tone
    So fit as thine to falter forth a sorrow:
Dost think men would go mad without a moan,
    If they knew any way to borrow
A pathos like thy own?

IV

"Which sigh wouldst mock, of all the sighs? The one
    So long escaping from lips starved and blue,
That lasts while on her pallet-bed the nun
    Stretches her length; her foot comes through
The straw she shivers on;

V

"You had not thought she was so tall: and spent,
    Her shrunk lids open, her lean fingers shut
Close, close, their sharp and livid nails indent
    The clammy palm; then all is mute:
That way, the spirit went.

VI

"Or wouldst thou rather that I understand
    Thy will to help me?—like the dog I found
Once, pacing sad this solitary strand,

Who would not take my food, poor hound,
But whined and licked my hand."

◆ ◆

VII

All this, and more, comes from some young man's pride
  Of power to see,—in failure and mistake,
Relinquishment, disgrace, on every side,—
  Merely examples for his sake,
Helps to his path untried:

VIII

Instances he must—simply recognize?
  Oh, more than so!—must, with a learner's zeal,
Make doubly prominent, twice emphasize,
  By added touches that reveal
The god in babe's disguise.

IX

Oh, he knows what defeat means, and the rest!
  Himself the undefeated that shall be:
Failure, disgrace, he flings them you to test,—
  His triumph, in eternity
Too plainly manifest!

X

Whence, judge if he learn forthwith what the wind
  Means in its moaning—by the happy prompt
Instinctive way of youth, I mean; for kind
  Calm years, exacting their accompt
Of pain, mature the mind:

XI

And some midsummer morning, at the lull
   Just about daybreak, as he looks across
A sparkling foreign country, wonderful
   To the sea's edge for gloom and gloss,
Next minute must annul,—

XII

Then, when the wind begins among the vines,
   So low, so low, what shall it say but this?
"Here is the change beginning, here the lines
   Circumscribe beauty, set to bliss
The limit time assigns."

XIII

Nothing can be as it has been before;
   Better, so call it, only not the same.
To draw one beauty into our hearts' core,
   And keep it changeless! such our claim;
So answered,—Never more!

XIV

Simple? Why this is the old woe o' the world;
   Tune, to whose rise and fall we live and die.
Rise with it, then! Rejoice that man is hurled
   From change to change unceasingly,
His soul's wings never furled!

XV

That's a new question; still replies the fact,
   Nothing endures: the wind moans, saying so;
We moan in acquiescence: there's life's pact,
   Perhaps probation—do *I* know?
God does: endure his act!

XVI

Only, for man, how bitter not to grave
    On his soul's hands' palms one fair good wise thing
Just as he grasped it! For himself, death's wave;
    While time first washes—ah, the sting!—
O'er all he'd sink to save.

VII. AMONG THE ROCKS

I

Oh, good gigantic smile o' the brown old earth,
    This autumn morning! How he sets his bones
To bask i' the sun, and thrusts out knees and feet
For the ripple to run over in its mirth;
    Listening the while, where on the heap of stones
The white breast of the sea-lark twitters sweet.

II

That is the doctrine, simple, ancient, true;
    Such is life's trial, as old earth smiles and knows.
If you loved only what were worth your love,
Love were clear gain, and wholly well for you:
    Make the low nature better by your throes!
Give earth yourself, go up for gain above!

VIII. BESIDE THE DRAWING-BOARD

I

"As like as a Hand to another Hand!"
    Whoever said that foolish thing,
Could not have studied to understand
    The counsels of God in fashioning,

Out of the infinite love of his heart,
This Hand, whose beauty I praise, apart
From the world of wonder left to praise,
If I tried to learn the other ways
Of love in its skill, or love in its power.
   "As like as a Hand to another Hand":
   Who said that, never took his stand,
Found and followed, like me, an hour,
The beauty in this,—how free, how fine
To fear, almost,—of the limit-line!
As I looked at this, and learned and drew,
   Drew and learned, and looked again,
While fast the happy minutes flew,
   Its beauty mounted into my brain,
   And a fancy seized me; I was fain
To efface my work, begin anew,
Kiss what before I only drew;
Ay, laying the red chalk 'twixt my lips,
   With soul to help if the mere lips failed,
   I kissed all right where the drawing ailed,
Kissed fast the grace that somehow slips
Still from one's soul-less finger-tips.

                    II
'Tis a clay cast, the perfect thing,
   From Hand live once, dead long ago:
Princess-like it wears the ring
   To fancy's eye, by which we know
That here at length a master found
   His match, a proud lone soul its mate,
As soaring genius sank to ground,
   And pencil could not emulate
The beauty in this,—how free, how fine
To fear almost!—of the limit-line.

Long ago the god, like me
The worm, learned, each in our degree:
Looked and loved, learned and drew,
   Drew and learned and loved again,
While fast the happy minutes flew,
   Till beauty mounted into his brain
And on the finger which outvied
   His art he placed the ring that's there,
Still by fancy's eye descried,
   In token of a marriage rare:
For him on earth, his art's despair,
For him in heaven, his soul's fit bride.

III

Little girl with the poor coarse hand
   I turned from to a cold clay cast—
I have my lesson, understand
   The worth of flesh and blood at last.
Nothing but beauty in a Hand?
   Because he could not change the hue,
   Mend the lines and make them true
To this which met his soul's demand,—
   Would Da Vinci turn from you?
I hear him laugh my woes to scorn—
"The fool forsooth is all forlorn
Because the beauty, she thinks best,
Lived long ago or was never born,—
Because no beauty bears the test
In this rough peasant Hand! Confessed!
'Art is null and study void!'
   So sayest thou? So said not I,
   Who threw the faulty pencil by,
And years instead of hours employed,
Learning the veritable use

Of flesh and bone and nerve beneath
Lines and hue of the outer sheath,
If haply I might reproduce
One motive of the powers profuse,
Flesh and bone and nerve that make
The poorest coarsest human hand
An object worthy to be scanned
A whole life long for their sole sake.
Shall earth and the cramped moment-space
Yield the heavenly crowning grace?
Now the parts and then the whole!
Who art thou, with stinted soul
And stunted body, thus to cry
"I love,—shall that be life's strait dole?
I must live beloved or die!"
This peasant hand that spins the wool
And bakes the bread, why lives it on,
Poor and coarse with beauty gone,—
What use survives the beauty?" Fool!

Go, little girl with the poor coarse hand!
I have my lesson, shall understand.

IX. ON DECK

I

There is nothing to remember in me,
Nothing I ever said with a grace,
Nothing I did that you care to see,
Nothing I was that deserves a place
In your mind, now I leave you, set you free.

II

Conceded! In turn, concede to me,
    Such things have been as a mutual flame.
Your soul's locked fast; but, love for a key,
    You might let it loose, till I grew the same
In your eyes, as in mine you stand: strange plea!

III

For then, then, what would it matter to me
    That I was the harsh ill-favoured one?
We both should be like as pea and pea;
    It was ever so since the world begun:
So, let me proceed with my reverie.

IV

How strange it were if you had all me,
    As I have all you in my heart and brain,
You, whose least word brought gloom or glee,
    Who never lifted the hand in vain—
Will hold mine yet, from over the sea!

V

Strange, if a face, when you thought of me,
    Rose like your own face present now,
With eyes as dear in their due degree,
    Much such a mouth, and as bright a brow,
Till you saw yourself, while you cried " 'Tis She!"

VI

Well, you may, you must, set down to me
    Love that was life, life that was love;
A tenure of breath at your lips' decree,
    A passion to stand as your thoughts approve,
A rapture to fall where your foot might be.

VII

But did one touch of such love for me
  Come in a word or a look of yours,
Whose words and looks will, circling, flee
  Round me and round while life endures,—
Could I fancy "As I feel, thus feels he";

VIII

Why, fade you might to a thing like me,
  And your hair grow these coarse hanks of hair,
Your skin, this bark of a gnarled tree,—
  You might turn myself!—should I know or care
When I should be dead of joy, James Lee?

The Worst of It

I

Would it were I had been false, not you!
  I that am nothing, not you that are all:
I, never the worse for a touch or two
  On my speckled hide; not you, the pride
Of the day, my swan, that a first fleck's fall
  On her wonder of white must unswan, undo!

II

I had dipped in life's struggle and, out again,
  Bore specks of it here, there, easy to see,
When I found my swan and the cure was plain;
  The dull turned bright as I caught your white
On my bosom: you saved me—saved in vain
  If you ruined yourself, and all through me!

III

Yes, all through the speckled beast that I am,
   Who taught you to stoop; you gave me yourself,
And bound your soul by the vows that damn:
   Since on better thought you break, as you ought,
Vows—words, no angel set down, some self
   Mistook,—for an oath, an epigram!

IV

Yes, might I judge you, here were my heart,
   And a hundred its like, to treat as you pleased!
I choose to be yours, for my proper part,
   Yours, leave or take, or mar me or make;
If I acquiesce, why should you be teased
   With the conscience-prick and the memory-smart?

V

But what will God say? Oh, my sweet,
   Think, and be sorry you did this thing
Though earth were unworthy to feel your feet,
   There's a heaven above may deserve your love:
Should you forfeit heaven for a snapt gold ring
   And a promise broke, were it just or meet?

VI

And I to have tempted you! I, who tried
   Your soul, no doubt, till it sank! Unwise,
I loved and was lowly, loved and aspired,
   Loved, grieving or glad, till I made you mad,
And you meant to have hated and despised—
   Whereas, you deceived me nor inquired!

VII

She, ruined? How? No heaven for her?
   Crowns to give, and none for the brow

That looked like marble and smelt like myrrh?
    Shall the robe be worn, and the palm-branch borne,
And she go graceless, she graced now
    Beyond all saints, as themselves aver?

VIII

Hardly! That must be understood!
    The earth is your place of penance, then;
And what will it prove? I desire your good,
    But, plot as I may, I can find no way
How a blow should fall, such as falls on men,
    Nor prove too much for your womanhood.

IX

It will come, I suspect, at the end of life,
    When you walk alone, and review the past;
And I, who so long shall have done with strife,
    And journeyed my stage and earned my wage
And retired as was right,—I am called at last
    When the devil stabs you, to lend the knife.

X

He stabs for the minute of trivial wrong,
    Nor the other hours are able to save,
The happy, that lasted my whole life long:
    For a promise broke, not for first words spoke,
The true, the only, that turn my grave
    To a blaze of joy and a crash of song.

XI

Witness beforehand! Off I trip
    On a safe path gay through the flowers you flung:
My very name made great by your lip,
    And my heart a-glow with the good I know

Of a perfect year when we both were young,
　　And I tasted the angels' fellowship.

XII

And witness, moreover . . . Ah, but wait!
　　I spy the loop whence an arrow shoots!
It may be for yourself, when you meditate,
　　That you grieve—for slain ruth, murdered truth.
"Though falsehood escape in the end, what boots?
　　How truth would have triumphed!"—you sigh too late.

XIII

Ay, who would have triumphed like you, I say!
　　Well, it is lost now; well, you must bear,
Abide and grow fit for a better day:
　　You should hardly grudge, could I be your judge!
But hush! For you, can be no despair:
　　There's amends: 'tis a secret: hope and pray!

XIV

For I was true at least—oh, true enough!
　　And, Dear, truth is not as good as it seems!
Commend me to conscience! Idle stuff!
　　Much help is in mine, as I mope and pine,
And skulk through day, and scowl in my dreams
　　At my swan's obtaining the crow's rebuff.

XV

Men tell me of truth now—"False!" I cry:
　　Of beauty—"A mask, friend! Look beneath!"
We take our own method, the devil and I,
　　With pleasant and fair and wise and rare:
And the best we wish to what lives, is—death;
　　Which even in wishing, perhaps we lie!

XVI

Far better commit a fault and have done—
 As you, Dear!—for ever; and choose the pure,
And look where the healing waters run,
 And strive and strain to be good again,
And a place in the other world ensure,
 All glass and gold, with God for its sun.

XVII

Misery! What shall I say or do?
 I cannot advise, or, at least, persuade:
Most like, you are glad you deceived me—rue
 No whit of the wrong: you endured too long,
Have done no evil and want no aid,
 Will live the old life out and chance the new.

XVIII

And your sentence is written all the same,
 And I can do nothing,—pray, perhaps:
But somehow the world pursues its game,—
 If I pray, if I curse,—for better or worse:
And my faith is torn to a thousand scraps,
 And my heart feels ice while my words breathe flame.

XIX

Dear, I look from my hiding-place.
 Are you still so fair? Have you still the eyes?
Be happy! Add but the other grace,
 Be good! Why want what the angels vaunt?
I knew you once: but in Paradise,
 If we meet, I will pass nor turn my face.

Too Late

I

Here was I with my arm and heart
   And brain, all yours for a word, a want
Put into a look—just a look, your part,—
   While mine, to repay it . . . vainest vaunt,
Were the woman, that's dead, alive to hear,
   Had her lover, that's lost, love's proof to show!
But I cannot show it; you cannot speak
   From the churchyard neither, miles removed,
Though I feel by a pulse within my cheek,
   Which stabs and stops, that the woman I loved
Needs help in her grave and finds none near,
   Wants warmth from the heart which sends it—so!

II

Did I speak once angrily, all the drear days
   You lived, you woman I loved so well,
Who married the other? Blame or praise,
   Where was the use then? Time would tell,
And the end declare what man for you,
   What woman for me, was the choice of God.
But, Edith dead! no doubting more!
   I used to sit and look at my life
As it rippled and ran till, right before,
   A great stone stopped it: oh, the strife
Of waves at the stone some devil threw
   In my life's midcurrent, thwarting God!

III

But either I thought, "They may churn and chide
   Awhile, my waves which came for their joy
And found this horrible stone full-tide:

Yet I see just a thread escape, deploy
Through the evening-country, silent and safe,
   And it suffers no more till it finds the sea."
Or else I would think, "Perhaps some night
   When new things happen, a meteor-ball
May slip through the sky in a line of light,
   And earth breathe hard, and landmarks fall,
And my waves no longer champ nor chafe,
   Since a stone will have rolled from its place: let be!"

IV

But, dead! All's done with: wait who may,
   Watch and wear and wonder who will.
Oh, my whole life that ends today!
   Oh, my soul's sentence, sounding still,
"The woman is dead that was none of his;
   And the man that was none of hers may go!"
There's only the past left: worry that!
   Wreak, like a bull, on the empty coat,
Rage, its late wearer is laughing at!
   Tear the collar to rags, having missed his throat;
Strike stupidly on—"This, this and this,
   Where I would that a bosom received the blow!"

V

I ought to have done more: once my speech,
   And once your answer, and there, the end,
And Edith was henceforth out of reach!
   Why, men do more to deserve a friend,
Be rid of a foe, get rich, grow wise,
   Nor, folding their arms, stare fate in the face.
Why, better even have burst like a thief
   And borne you away to a rock for us two,
In a moment's horror, bright, bloody and brief:

Then changed to myself again—"I slew
Myself in that moment; a ruffian lies
    Somewhere: your slave, see, born in his place!"

VI

What did the other do? You be judge!
    Look at us, Edith! Here are we both!
Give him his six whole years: I grudge
    None of the life with you, nay, loathe
Myself that I grudged his start in advance
    Of me who could overtake and pass.
But, as if he loved you! No, not he,
    Nor anyone else in the world, 'tis plain:
Who ever heard that another, free
    As I, young, prosperous, sound and sane,
Poured life out, proffered it—"Half a glance
    Of those eyes of yours and I drop the glass!"

VII

Handsome, were you? 'Tis more than they held,
    More than they said; I was 'ware and watched:
I was the 'scapegrace, this rat belled
    The cat, this fool got his whiskers scratched:
The others? No head that was turned, no heart
    Broken, my lady, assure yourself!
Each soon made his mind up; so and so
    Married a dancer, such and such
Stole his friend's wife, stagnated slow,
    Or maundered, unable to do as much,
And muttered of peace where he had no part:
    While, hid in the closet, laid on the shelf,—

VIII

On the whole, you were let alone, I think!
    So, you looked to the other, who acquiesced;
My rival, the proud man,—prize your pink
    Of poets! A poet he was! I've guessed:
He rhymed you his rubbish nobody read,
    Loved you and doved you—did not I laugh!
There was a prize! But we both were tried.
    Oh, heart of mine, marked broad with her mark,
Tekel, found wanting, set aside,
    Scorned! See, I bleed these tears in the dark
Till comfort come and the last be bled:
    He? He is tagging your epitaph.

IX

If it would only come over again!
    —Time to be patient with me, and probe
This heart till you punctured the proper vein,
    Just to learn what blood is: twitch the robe
From that blank lay-figure your fancy draped,
    Prick the leathern heart till the—verses spurt!
And late it was easy; late, you walked
    Where a friend might meet you; Edith's name
Arose to one's lip if one laughed or talked;
    If I heard good news, you heard the same;
When I woke, I knew that your breath escaped;
    I could bide my time, keep alive, alert.

X

And alive I shall keep and long, you will see!
    I knew a man, was kicked like a dog
From gutter to cesspool; what cared he
    So long as he picked from the filth his prog?
He saw youth, beauty and genius die,
    And jollily lived to his hundredth year.

But I will live otherwise: none of such life!
　　At once I begin as I mean to end.
Go on with the world, get gold in its strife,
　　Give your spouse the slip and betray your friend!
There are two who decline, a woman and I,
　　And enjoy our death in the darkness here.

XI

I liked that way you had with your curls
　　Wound to a ball in a net behind:
Your cheek was chaste as a quaker-girl's,
　　And your mouth—there was never, to my mind,
Such a funny mouth, for it would not shut;
　　And the dented chin too—what a chin!
There were certain ways when you spoke, some words
　　That you know you never could pronounce:
You were thin, however; like a bird's
　　Your hand seemed—some would say, the pounce
Of a scaly-footed hawk—all but!
　　The world was right when it called you thin.

XII

But I turn my back on the world: I take
　　Your hand, and kneel, and lay to my lips.
Bid me live, Edith! Let me slake
　　Thirst at your presence! Fear no slips:
'Tis your slave shall pay, while his soul endures,
　　Full due, love's whole debt, *summum jus*.
My queen shall have high observance, planned
　　Courtship made perfect, no least line
Crossed without warrant. There you stand,
　　Warm too, and white too: would this wine
Had washed all over that body of yours,
　　Ere I drank it, and you down with it, thus!

Abt Vogler

*(After he has been extemporizing
upon the musical instrument of his invention)*

I

Would that the structure brave, the manifold music I build,
  Bidding my organ obey, calling its keys to their work,
Claiming each slave of the sound, at a touch, as when Solomon
    willed
  Armies of angels that soar, legions of demons that lurk,
Man, brute, reptile, fly,—alien of end and of aim,
  Adverse, each from the other heaven-high, hell-deep removed,—
Should rush into sight at once as he named the ineffable Name,
  And pile him a palace straight, to pleasure the princess he loved!

II

Would it might tarry like his, the beautiful building of mine,
  This which my keys in a crowd pressed and importuned to raise!
Ah, one and all, how they helped, would dispart now and now
    combine,
  Zealous to hasten the work, heighten their master his praise!
And one would bury his brow with a blind plunge down to hell,
  Burrow awhile and build, broad on the roots of things,
Then up again swim into sight, having based me my palace well,
  Founded it, fearless of flame, flat on the nether springs.

III

And another would mount and march, like the excellent minion he
    was,
  Ay, another and yet another, one crowd but with many a crest,
Raising my rampired walls of gold as transparent as glass,
  Eager to do and die, yield each his place to the rest:
For higher still and higher (as a runner tips with fire,
  When a great illumination surprises a festal night—

Outlining round and round Rome's dome from space to spire)
  Up, the pinnacled glory reached, and the pride of my soul was
    in sight.

IV

In sight? Not half! for it seemed, it was certain, to match man's
    birth,
  Nature in turn conceived, obeying an impulse as I;
And the emulous heaven yearned down, made effort to reach the
    earth,
  As the earth had done her best, in my passion, to scale the sky:
Novel splendours burst forth, grew familiar and dwelt with mine,
  Not a point nor peak but found and fixed its wandering star;
Meteor-moons, balls of blaze: and they did not pale nor pine,
  For earth had attained to heaven, there was no more near nor
    far.

V

Nay more; for there wanted not who walked in the glare and
    glow,
  Presences plain in the place; or, fresh from the Protoplast,
Furnished for ages to come, when a kindlier wind should blow,
  Lured now to begin and live, in a house to their liking at last;
Or else the wonderful Dead who have passed through the body and
    gone,
  But were back once more to breathe in an old world worth their
    new:
What never had been, was now; what was, as it shall be anon;
  And what is,—shall I say, matched both? for I was made perfect
    too.

VI

All through my keys that gave their sounds to a wish of my soul,
  All through my soul that praised as its wish flowed visibly forth,
All through music and me! For think, had I painted the whole,

Why, there it had stood, to see, nor the process so
    wonder-worth:
Had I written the same, made verse—still, effect proceeds from
    cause,
    Ye know why the forms are fair, ye hear how the tale is told;
It is all triumphant art, but art in obedience to laws,
    Painter and poet are proud in the artist-list enrolled:—

VII

But here is the finger of God, a flash of the will that can,
    Existent behind all laws, that made them and, lo, they are!
And I know not if, save in this, such gift be allowed to man,
    That out of three sounds he frame, not a fourth sound, but a
        star.
Consider it well: each tone of our scale in itself is naught;
    It is everywhere in the world—loud, soft, and all is said:
Give it to me to use! I mix it with two in my thought:
    And, there! Ye have heard and seen: consider and bow the head!

VIII

Well, it is gone at last, the palace of music I reared;
    Gone! and the good tears start, the praises that come too slow;
For one is assured at first, one scarce can say that he feared,
    That he even gave it a thought, the gone thing was to go.
Never to be again! But many more of the kind
    As good, nay, better perchance: is this your comfort to me?
To me, who must be saved because I cling with my mind
    To the same, same self, same love, same God: ay, what was, shall
        be.

IX

Therefore to whom turn I but to thee, the ineffable Name?
    Builder and maker, thou, of houses not made with hands!
What, have fear of change from thee who art ever the same?

Doubt that thy power can fill the heart that thy power expands?
There shall never be one lost good! What was, shall live as before;
 The evil is null, is naught, is silence implying sound;
What was good shall be good, with, for evil, so much good more;
 On the earth the broken arcs; in the heaven, a perfect round.

X

All we have willed or hoped or dreamed of good shall exist;
 Not its semblance, but itself; no beauty, nor good, nor power
Whose voice has gone forth, but each survives for the melodist
 When eternity affirms the conception of an hour.
The high that proved too high, the heroic for earth too hard,
 The passion that left the ground to lose itself in the sky,
Are music sent up to God by the lover and the bard;
 Enough that he heard it once: we shall hear it by-and-by.

XI

And what is our failure here but a triumph's evidence
 For the fulness of the days? Have we withered or agonized?
Why else was the pause prolonged but that singing might issue
      thence?
 Why rushed the discords in but that harmony should be prized?
Sorrow is hard to bear, and doubt is slow to clear,
 Each sufferer says his say, his scheme of the weal and woe:
But God has a few of us whom he whispers in the ear;
 The rest may reason and welcome: 'tis we musicians know.

XII

Well, it is earth with me; silence resumes her reign:
 I will be patient and proud, and soberly acquiesce.
Give me the keys. I feel for the common chord again,
 Sliding by semitones, till I sink to the minor,—yes,
And I blunt it into a ninth, and I stand on alien ground,
 Surveying awhile the heights I rolled from into the deep;

Which, hark, I have dared and done, for my resting-place is found,
The C Major of this life: so, now I will try to sleep.

Caliban upon Setebos; or, Natural Theology in the Island

"Thou thoughtest that I was altogether such a one as thyself."

['Will sprawl, now that the heat of day is best,
Flat on his belly in the pit's much mire,
With elbows wide, fists clenched to prop his chin.
And, while he kicks both feet in the cool slush,
And feels about his spine small eft-things course,
Run in and out each arm, and make him laugh:
And while above his head a pompion-plant,
Coating the cave-top as a brow its eye,
Creeps down to touch and tickle hair and beard,
And now a flower drops with a bee inside,
And now a fruit to snap at, catch and crunch,—
He looks out o'er yon sea which sunbeams cross
And recross till they weave a spider-web
(Meshes of fire, some great fish breaks at times)
And talks to his own self, howe'er he please,
Touching that other, whom his dam called God.
Because to talk about Him, vexes—ha,
Could He but know! and time to vex is now,
When talk is safer than in winter-time.
Moreover Prosper and Miranda sleep
In confidence he drudges at their task,
And it is good to cheat the pair, and gibe,
Letting the rank tongue blossom into speech.]

Setebos, Setebos, and Setebos!
'Thinketh, He dwelleth i' the cold o' the moon.

'Thinketh He made it, with the sun to match,
But not the stars; the stars came otherwise;
Only made clouds, winds, meteors, such as that:
Also this isle, what lives and grows thereon,
And snaky sea which rounds and ends the same.

'Thinketh, it came of being ill at ease:
He hated that He cannot change His cold,
Nor cure its ache. 'Hath spied an icy fish
That longed to 'scape the rock-stream where she lived,
And thaw herself within the lukewarm brine
O' the lazy sea her stream thrusts far amid,
A crystal spike 'twixt two warm walls of wave;
Only, she ever sickened, found repulse
At the other kind of water, not her life,
(Green-dense and dim-delicious, bred o' the sun)
Flounced back from bliss she was not born to breathe,
And in her old bounds buried her despair,
Hating and loving warmth alike: so He.

'Thinketh, He made thereat the sun, this isle,
Trees and the fowls here, beast and creeping thing.
Yon otter, sleek-wet, black, lithe as a leech;
Yon auk, one fire-eye in a ball of foam,
That floats and feeds; a certain badger brown
He hath watched hunt with that slant white-wedge eye
By moonlight; and the pie with the long tongue
That pricks deep into oakwarts for a worm,
And says a plain word when she finds her prize,
But will not eat the ants; the ants themselves
That build a wall of seeds and settled stalks
About their hole—He made all these and more,
Made all we see, and us, in spite: how else?
He could not, Himself, make a second self

To be His mate; as well have made Himself:
He would not make what he mislikes or slights,
An eyesore to Him, or not worth His pains:
But did, in envy, listlessness or sport,
Make what Himself would fain, in a manner, be—
Weaker in most points, stronger in a few,
Worthy, and yet mere playthings all the while,
Things He admires and mocks too,—that is it.
Because, so brave, so better though they be,
It nothing skills if He begin to plague.
Look now, I melt a gourd-fruit into mash,
Add honeycomb and pods, I have perceived,
Which bite like finches when they bill and kiss,—
Then, when froth rises bladdery, drink up all,
Quick, quick, till maggots scamper through my brain;
Last, throw me on my back i' the seeded thyme,
And wanton, wishing I were born a bird.
Put case, unable to be what I wish,
I yet could make a live bird out of clay:
Would not I take clay, pinch my Caliban
Able to fly?—for, there, see, he hath wings,
And great comb like the hoopoe's to admire,
And there, a sting to do his foes offence,
There, and I will that he begin to live,
Fly to yon rock-top, nip me off the horns
Of grigs high up that make the merry din,
Saucy through their veined wings, and mind me not.
In which feat, if his leg snapped, brittle clay,
And he lay stupid-like,—why, I should laugh;
And if he, spying me, should fall to weep,
Beseech me to be good, repair his wrong,
Bid his poor leg smart less or grow again,—
Well, as the chance were, this might take or else
Not take my fancy: I might hear his cry,

And give the mankin three sound legs for one,
Or pluck the other off, leave him like an egg,
And lessoned he was mine and merely clay.
Were this no pleasure, lying in the thyme,
Drinking the mash, with brain become alive,
Making and marring clay at will? So He.

'Thinketh, such shows nor right nor wrong in Him,
Nor kind, nor cruel: He is strong and Lord.
'Am strong myself compared to yonder crabs
That march now from the mountain to the sea,
'Let twenty pass, and stone the twenty-first,
Loving not, hating not, just choosing so.
'Say, the first straggler that boasts purple spots
Shall join the file, one pincer twisted off;
'Say, this bruised fellow shall receive a worm,
And two worms he whose nippers end in red;
As it likes me each time, I do: so He.

Well then, 'supposeth He is good i' the main,
Placable if His mind and ways were guessed,
But rougher than His handiwork, be sure!
Oh, He hath made things worthier than Himself,
And envieth that, so helped, such things do more
Than He who made them! What consoles but this?
That they, unless through Him, do naught at all,
And must submit: what other use in things?
'Hath cut a pipe of pithless elder-joint
That, blown through, gives exact the scream o' the jay
When from her wing you twitch the feathers blue:
Sound this, and little birds that hate the jay
Flock within stone's throw, glad their foe is hurt:
Put case such pipe could prattle and boast forsooth
"I catch the birds, I am the crafty thing,

I make the cry my maker cannot make
With his great round mouth; he must blow through mine!"
Would not I smash it with my foot? So He.

But wherefore rough, why cold and ill at ease?
Aha, that is a question! Ask, for that,
What knows,—the something over Setebos
That made Him, or He, may be, found and fought,
Worsted, drove off and did to nothing, perchance.
There may be something quiet o'er His head,
Out of His reach, that feels nor joy nor grief,
Since both derive from weakness in some way.
I joy because the quails come; would not joy
Could I bring quails here when I have a mind:
This Quiet, all it hath a mind to, doth.
'Esteemeth stars the outposts of its couch,
But never spends much thought nor care that way.
It may look up, work up,—the worse for those
It works on! 'Careth but for Setebos
The many-handed as a cuttle-fish,
Who, making Himself feared through what He does,
Looks up, first, and perceives he cannot soar
To what is quiet and hath happy life;
Next looks down here, and out of very spite
Makes this a bauble-world to ape yon real,
These good things to match those as hips do grapes.
'Tis solace making baubles, ay, and sport.
Himself peeped late, eyed Prosper at his books
Careless and lofty, lord now of the isle:
Vexed, 'stitched a book of broad leaves, arrow-shaped,
Wrote thereon, he knows what, prodigious words;
Has peeled a wand and called it by a name;
Weareth at whiles for an enchanter's robe
The eyed skin of a supple oncelot;

And hath an ounce sleeker than youngling mole,
A four-legged serpent he makes cower and couch,
Now snarl, now hold its breath and mind his eye,
And saith she is Miranda and my wife:
'Keeps for his Ariel a tall pouch-bill crane
He bids go wade for fish and straight disgorge;
Also a sea-beast, lumpish, which he snared,
Blinded the eyes of, and brought somewhat tame,
And split its toe-webs, and now pens the drudge
In a hole o' the rock and calls him Caliban;
A bitter heart that bides its time and bites.
'Plays thus at being Prosper in a way,
Taketh his mirth with make-believes: so He.

His dam held that the Quiet made all things
Which Setebos vexed only: 'holds not so.
Who made them weak, meant weakness He might vex.
Had He meant other, while His hand was in,
Why not make horny eyes no thorn could prick,
Or plate my scalp with bone against the snow,
Or overscale my flesh 'neath joint and joint,
Like an orc's armour? Ay,—so spoil His sport!
He is the One now: only He doth all.

'Saith, He may like, perchance, what profits Him.
Ay, himself loves what does him good; but why?
'Gets good no otherwise. This blinded beast
Loves whoso places flesh-meat on his nose,
But, had he eyes, would want no help, but hate
Or love, just as it liked him: He hath eyes.
Also it pleaseth Setebos to work,
Use all His hands, and exercise much craft,
By no means for the love of what is worked.
'Tasteth, himself, no finer good i' the world

When all goes right, in this safe summer-time,
And he wants little, hungers, aches not much,
Than trying what to do with wit and strength.
'Falls to make something: 'piled yon pile of turfs,
And squared and stuck there squares of soft white chalk,
And, with a fish-tooth, scratched a moon on each,
And set up endwise certain spikes of tree,
And crowned the whole with a sloth's skull a-top,
Found dead i' the woods, too hard for one to kill.
No use at all i' the work, for work's sole sake;
'Shall some day knock it down again: so He.

'Saith He is terrible: watch His feats in proof!
One hurricane will spoil six good months' hope.
He hath a spite against me, that I know,
Just as He favours Prosper, who knows why?
So it is, all the same, as well I find.
'Wove wattles half the winter, fenced them firm
With stone and stake to stop she-tortoises
Crawling to lay their eggs here: well, one wave,
Feeling the foot of Him upon its neck,
Gaped as a snake does, lolled out its large tongue,
And licked the whole labour flat: so much for spite.
'Saw a ball flame down late (yonder it lies)
Where, half an hour before, I slept i' the shade:
Often they scatter sparkles: there is force!
'Dug up a newt He may have envied once
And turned to stone, shut up inside a stone.
Please Him and hinder this?—What Prosper does?
Aha, if He would tell me how! Not He!
There is the sport: discover how or die!
All need not die, for of the things o' the isle
Some flee afar, some dive, some run up trees;
Those at His mercy,—why, they please Him most

When . . . when . . . well, never try the same way twice!
Repeat what act has pleased, He may grow wroth.
You must not know His ways, and play Him off,
Sure of the issue. 'Doth the like himself:
'Spareth a squirrel that it nothing fears
But steals the nut from underneath my thumb,
And when I threat, bites stoutly in defence:
'Spareth an urchin that contrariwise,
Curls up into a ball, pretending death
For fright at my approach: the two ways please.
But what would move my choler more than this,
That either creature counted on its life
Tomorrow and next day and all days to come,
Saying, forsooth, in the inmost of its heart,
"Because he did so yesterday with me,
And otherwise with such another brute,
So must he do henceforth and always."—Ay?
Would teach the reasoning couple what "must" means!
'Doth as he likes, or wherefore Lord? So He.

'Conceiveth all things will continue thus,
And we shall have to live in fear of Him
So long as He lives, keeps His strength: no change,
If He have done His best, make no new world
To please Him more, so leave off watching this,—
If He surprise not even the Quiet's self
Some strange day,—or, suppose, grow into it
As grubs grow butterflies: else, here are we,
And there is He, and nowhere help at all.

'Believeth with the life, the pain shall stop.
His dam held different, that after death
He both plagued enemies and feasted friends:
Idly! He doth His worst in this our life,

Giving just respite lest we die through pain,
Saving last pain for worst,—with which, an end.
Meanwhile, the best way to escape His ire
Is, not to seem too happy. 'Sees, himself,
Yonder two flies, with purple films and pink,
Bask on the pompion-bell above: kills both.
'Sees two black painful beetles roll their ball
On head and tail as if to save their lives:
Moves them the stick away they strive to clear.

Even so, 'would have Him misconceive, suppose
This Caliban strives hard and ails no less,
And always, above all else, envies Him;
Wherefore he mainly dances on dark nights,
Moans in the sun, gets under holes to laugh,
And never speaks his mind save housed as now:
Outside, 'groans, curses. If He caught me here,
O'erheard this speech, and asked "What chucklest at?"
'Would, to appease Him, cut a finger off,
Or of my three kid yearlings burn the best,
Or let the toothsome apples rot on tree,
Or push my tame beast for the orc to taste:
While myself lit a fire, and made a song
And sung it, *"What I hate, be consecrate*
To celebrate Thee and Thy state, no mate
For Thee; what see for envy in poor me?"
Hoping the while, since evils sometimes mend,
Warts rub away and sores are cured with slime,
That some strange day, will either the Quiet catch
And conquer Setebos, or likelier He
Decrepit may doze, doze, as good as die.
[What, what? A curtain o'er the world at once!
Crickets stop hissing; not a bird—or, yes,
There scuds His raven that has told Him all!

It was fool's play, this prattling! Ha! The wind
Shoulders the pillared dust, death's house o' the move,
And fast invading fires begin! White blaze—
A tree's head snaps—and there, there, there, there, there,
His thunder follows! Fool to gibe at Him!
Lo! 'Lieth flat and loveth Setebos!
'Maketh his teeth meet through his upper lip,
Will let those quails fly, will not eat this month
One little mess of whelks, so he may 'scape!]

FROM *PACCHIAROTTO AND HOW HE WORKED IN DISTEMPER eT cETERA,* 1876

At the "Mermaid"

The figure that thou here seest . . . Tut!
Was it for gentle Shakespeare put?
B. JONSON *(adapted)*

I

I—"Next Poet?" No, my hearties,
   I nor am nor fain would be!
Choose your chiefs and pick your parties,
   Not one soul revolt to me!
I, forsooth, sow song-sedition?
   I, a schism in verse provoke?
I, blown up by bard's ambition,
   Burst—your bubble-king? You joke.

II

Come, be grave! The sherris mantling
   Still about each mouth, mayhap,
Breeds you insight—just a scantling—
   Brings me truth out—just a scrap.

Look and tell me! Written, spoken,
　　Here's my life-long work: and where
—Where's your warrant or my token
　　I'm the dead king's son and heir?

III

Here's my work: does work discover—
　　What was rest from work—my life?
Did I live man's hater, lover?
　　Leave the world at peace, at strife?
Call earth ugliness or beauty?
　　See things there in large or small?
Use to pay its Lord my duty?
　　Use to own a lord at all?

IV

Blank of such a record, truly
　　Here's the work I hand, this scroll,
Yours to take or leave; as duly,
　　Mine remains the unproffered soul.
So much, no whit more, my debtors—
　　How should one like me lay claim
To that largess elders, betters
　　Sell you cheap their souls for—fame?

V

Which of you did I enable
　　Once to slip inside my breast,
There to catalogue and label
　　What I like least, what love best,
Hope and fear, believe and doubt of,
　　Seek and shun, respect—deride?
Who has right to make a rout of
　　Rarities he found inside?

VI

Rarities or, as he'd rather,
    Rubbish such as stocks his own:
Need and greed (O strange) the Father
    Fashioned not for him alone!
Whence—the comfort set a-strutting,
    Whence—the outcry "Haste, behold!
Bard's breast open wide, past shutting,
    Shows what brass we took for gold!"

VII

Friends, I doubt not he'd display you
    Brass—myself call orichalc,—
Furnish much amusement; pray you
    Therefore, be content I balk
Him and you, and bar my portal!
    Here's my work outside: opine
What's inside me mean and mortal!
    Take your pleasure, leave me mine!

VIII

Which is—not to buy your laurel
    As last king did, nothing loth.
Tale adorned and pointed moral
    Gained him praise and pity both.
Out rushed sighs and groans by dozens,
    Forth by scores oaths, curses flew:
Proving you were cater-cousins,
    Kith and kindred, king and you!

IX

Whereas do I ne'er so little
    (Thanks to sherris) leave ajar
Bosom's gate—no jot nor tittle

Grow we nearer than we are.
Sinning, sorrowing, despairing,
   Body-ruined, spirit-wrecked,—
Should I give my woes an airing,—
   Where's one plague that claims respect?

X

Have you found your life distasteful?
   My life did, and does, smack sweet.
Was your youth of pleasure wasteful?
   Mine I saved and hold complete.
Do your joys with age diminish?
   When mine fail me, I'll complain.
Must in death your daylight finish?
   My sun sets to rise again.

XI

What, like you, he proved—your Pilgrim—
   This our world a wilderness,
Earth still grey and heaven still grim,
   Not a hand there his might press,
Not a heart his own might throb to,
   Men all rogues and women—say,
Dolls which boys' heads duck and bob to,
   Grown folk drop or throw away?

XII

My experience being other,
   How should I contribute verse
Worthy of your king and brother?
   Balaam-like I bless, not curse.
I find earth not grey but rosy,
   Heaven not grim but fair of hue.
Do I stoop? I pluck a posy.
   Do I stand and stare? All's blue.

XIII

Doubtless I am pushed and shoved by
    Rogues and fools enough: the more
Good luck mine, I love, am loved by
    Some few honest to the core.
Scan the near high, scout the far low!
    "But the low come close:" what then?
Simpletons? My match is Marlowe;
    Sciolists? My mate is Ben.

XIV

Womankind—"the cat-like nature,
    False and fickle, vain and weak"—
What of this sad nomenclature
    Suits my tongue, if I must speak?
Does the sex invite, repulse so,
    Tempt, betray, by fits and starts?
So becalm but to convulse so,
    Decking heads and breaking hearts?

XV

Well may you blaspheme at fortune!
    I "threw Venus" (Ben, expound!)
Never did I need importune
    Her, of all the Olympian round.
Blessings on my benefactress!
    Cursings suit—for aught I know—
Those who twitched her by the back tress,
    Tugged and thought to turn her—so!

XVI

Therefore, since no leg to stand on
    Thus I'm left with,—joy or grief
Be the issue,—I abandon
    Hope or care you name me Chief!

Chief and king and Lord's anointed,
    I?—who never once have wished
Death before the day appointed:
    Lived and liked, not poohed and pished!

XVII

"Ah, but so I shall not enter,
    Scroll in hand, the common heart—
Stopped at surface: since at centre
    Song should reach *Welt-schmerz,* world-smart!"
"Enter in the heart?" Its shelly
    Cuirass guard mine, fore and aft!
Such song "enters in the belly
    And is cast out in the draught."

XVIII

Back then to our sherris-brewage!
    "Kingship" quotha? I shall wait—
Waive the present time: some new age . . .
    But let fools anticipate!
Meanwhile greet me—"friend, good fellow,
    Gentle Will," my merry men!
As for making Envy yellow
    With "Next Poet"—(Manners, Ben!)

Numpholeptos

Still you stand, still you listen, still you smile!
Still melts your moonbeam through me, white awhile,
Softening, sweetening, till sweet and soft
Increase so round this heart of mine, that oft
I could believe your moonbeam-smile has past
The pallid limit, lies, transformed at last
To sunlight and salvation—warms the soul

It sweetens, softens! Would you pass that goal,
Gain love's birth at the limit's happier verge,
And, where an iridescence lurks, but urge
The hesitating pallor on to prime
Of dawn!—true blood-streaked, sun-warmth, action-time,
By heart-pulse ripened to a ruddy glow
Of gold above my clay—I scarce should know
From gold's self, thus suffused! For gold means love.
What means the sad slow silver smile above
My clay but pity, pardon?—at the best,
But acquiescence that I take my rest,
Contented to be clay, while in your heaven
The sun reserves love for the Spirit-Seven
Companioning God's throne they lamp before,
—Leaves earth a mute waste only wandered o'er
By that pale soft sweet disempassioned moon
Which smiles me slow forgiveness! Such the boon
I beg? Nay, dear, submit to this—just this
Supreme endeavour! As my lips now kiss
Your feet, my arms convulse your shrouding robe,
My eyes, acquainted with the dust, dare probe
Your eyes above for—what, if born, would blind
Mine with redundant bliss, as flash may find
The inert nerve, sting awake the palsied limb,
Bid with life's ecstasy sense overbrim
And suck back death in the resurging joy—
Love, the love whole and sole without alloy!

Vainly! The promise withers! I employ
Lips, arms, eyes, pray the prayer which finds the word,
Make the appeal which must be felt, not heard,
And none the more is changed your calm regard:
Rather, its sweet and soft grow harsh and hard—
Forbearance, then repulsion, then disdain.

Avert the rest! I rise, see!—make, again
Once more, the old departure for some track
Untried yet through a world which brings me back
Ever thus fruitlessly to find your feet,
To fix your eyes, to pray the soft and sweet
Which smile there—take from his new pilgrimage
Your outcast, once your inmate, and assuage
With love—not placid pardon now—his thirst
For a mere drop from out the ocean erst
He drank at! Well, the quest shall be renewed.
Fear nothing! Though I linger, unembued
With any drop, my lips thus close. I go!
So did I leave you, I have found you so,
And doubtlessly, if fated to return,
So shall my pleading persevere and earn
Pardon—not love—in that same smile, I learn,
And lose the meaning of, to learn once more,
Vainly!

What fairy track do I explore?
What magic hall return to, like the gem
Centuply-angled o'er a diadem?
You dwell there, hearted; from your midmost home
Rays forth—through that fantastic world I roam
Ever—from centre to circumference,
Shaft upon coloured shaft: this crimsons thence,
That purples out its precinct through the waste.
Surely I had your sanction when I faced,
Fared forth upon that untried yellow ray
Whence I retrack my steps? They end today
Where they began—before your feet, beneath
Your eyes, your smile: the blade is shut in sheath,
Fire quenched in flint; irradiation, late
Triumphant through the distance, finds its fate,

Merged in your blank pure soul, alike the source
And tomb of that prismatic glow: divorce
Absolute, all-conclusive! Forth I fared,
Treading the lambent flamelet: little cared
If now its flickering took the topaz tint,
If now my dull-caked path gave sulphury hint
Of subterranean rage—no stay nor stint
To yellow, since you sanctioned that I bathe,
Burnish me, soul and body, swim and swathe
In yellow license. Here I reek suffused
With crocus, saffron, orange, as I used
With scarlet, purple, every dye o' the bow
Born of the storm-cloud. As before, you show
Scarce recognition, no approval, some
Mistrust, more wonder at a man become
Monstrous in garb, nay—flesh disguised as well,
Through his adventure. Whatsoe'er befell,
I followed, whereso'er it wound, that vein
You authorized should leave your whiteness, stain
Earth's sombre stretch beyond your midmost place
Of vantage,—trode that tinct whereof the trace
On garb and flesh repel you! Yes, I plead
Your own permission—your command, indeed,
That who would worthily retain the love
Must share the knowledge shrined those eyes above,
Go boldly on adventure, break through bounds
O' the quintessential whiteness that surrounds
Your feet, obtain experience of each tinge
That bickers forth to broaden out, impinge
Plainer his foot its pathway all distinct
From every other. Ah, the wonder, linked
With fear, as exploration manifests
What agency it was first tipped the crests
Of unnamed wildflower, soon protruding grew

Portentous 'mid the sands, as when his hue
Betrays him and the burrowing snake gleams through;
Till, last . . . but why parade more shame and pain?
Are not the proofs upon me? Here again
I pass into your presence, I receive
Your smile of pity, pardon, and I leave . . .
No, not this last of times I leave you, mute,
Submitted to my penance, so my foot
May yet again adventure, tread, from source
To issue, one more ray of rays which course
Each other, at your bidding, from the sphere
Silver and sweet, their birthplace, down that drear
Dark of the world,—you promise shall return
Your pilgrim jewelled as with drops o' the urn
The rainbow paints from, and no smatch at all
Of ghastliness at edge of some cloud-pall
Heaven cowers before, as earth awaits the fall
O' the bolt and flash of doom. Who trusts your word
Tries the adventure: and returns—absurd
As frightful—in that sulphur-steeped disguise
Mocking the priestly cloth-of-gold, sole prize
The arch-heretic was wont to bear away
Until he reached the burning. No, I say:
No fresh adventure! No more seeking love
At end of toil, and finding, calm above
My passion, the old statuesque regard,
The sad petrific smile!

          O you—less hard
And hateful than mistaken and obtuse
Unreason of a she-intelligence!
You very woman with the pert pretence
To match the male achievement! Like enough!
Ay, you were easy victors, did the rough
Straightway efface itself to smooth, the gruff

Grind down and grow a whisper,—did man's truth
Subdue, for sake of chivalry and ruth,
Its rapier-edge to suit the bulrush-spear
Womanly falsehood fights with! O that ear
All fact pricks rudely, that thrice-superfine
Feminity of sense, with right divine
To waive all process, take result stain-free
From out the very muck wherein . . .

     Ah me!
The true slave's querulous outbreak! All the rest
Be resignation! Forth at your behest
I fare. Who knows but this—the crimson-quest—
May deepen to a sunrise, not decay
To that cold sad sweet smile?—which I obey.

FROM *LA SAISIAZ*, 1878

From *La Saisiaz*

A.E.S. 14 SEPTEMBER 1877

Dared and done: at last I stand upon the summit, Dear and True!
Singly dared and done; the climbing both of us were bound to do.
Petty feat and yet prodigious: every side my glance was bent
O'er the grandeur and the beauty lavished through the whole
    ascent.
Ledge by ledge, out broke new marvels, now minute and now
    immense:
Earth's most exquisite disclosure, heaven's own God in evidence!
And no berry in its hiding, no blue space in its outspread,
Pleaded to escape my footstep, challenged my emerging head,
(As I climbed or paused from climbing, now o'erbranched by shrub
    and tree,
Now built round by rock and boulder, now at just a turn set free

Stationed face to face with—Nature? rather with Infinitude)
—No revealment of them all, as singly I my path pursued,
But a bitter touched its sweetness, for the thought stung "Even so
Both of us had loved and wondered just the same, five days ago!"
Five short days, sufficient hardly to entice, from out its den
Splintered in the slab, this pink perfection of the cyclamen;
Scarce enough to heal and coat with amber gum the sloe-tree's
     gash,
Bronze the clustered wilding apple, redden ripe the mountain-ash:
Yet of might to place between us—Oh the barrier! Yon Profound
Shrinks beside it, proves a pin-point: barrier this, without a bound!

Boundless though it be, I reach you: somehow seem to have you
     here
—Who are there. Yes, there you dwell now, plain the four low
     walls appear;
Those are vineyards they enclose from; and the little spire which
     points
—That's Collonge, henceforth your dwelling. All the same, howe'er
     disjoints
Past from present, no less certain you are here, not there: have
     dared,
Done the feat of mountain-climbing,—five days since, we both
     prepared
Daring, doing, arm in arm, if other help should haply fail.
For you asked, as forth we sallied to see sunset from the vale,
"Why not try for once the mountain,—take a foretaste, snatch by
     stealth
Sight and sound, some unconsidered fragment of the hoarded
     wealth?
Six weeks at its base, yet never once have we together won
Sight or sound by honest climbing: let us two have dared and done
Just so much of twilight journey as may prove tomorrow's jaunt
Not the only mode of wayfare—wheeled to reach the eagle's
     haunt!"

So, we turned from the low grass-path you were pleased to call
   "your own,"
Set our faces to the rose-bloom o'er the summit's front of stone
Where Salève obtains, from Jura and the sunken sun she hides,
Due return of blushing "Good Night," rosy as a borne-off bride's,
For his masculine "Good Morrow" when, with sunrise still in hold,
Gay he hails her, and, magnific, thrilled her black length burns to
   gold.
Up and up we went, how careless—nay, how joyous! All was new,
All was strange. "Call progress toilsome? that were just insulting
   you!
How the trees must temper noontide! Ah, the thicket's sudden
   break!
What will be the morning glory, when at dusk thus gleams the
   lake?
Light by light puts forth Geneva: what a land—and, of the land,
Can there be a lovelier station than this spot where now we stand?
Is it late, and wrong to linger? True, tomorrow makes amends.
Toilsome progress? child's play, call it—specially when one
   descends!
There, the dread descent is over—hardly our adventure, though!
Take the vale where late we left it, pace the grass-path, "mine,"
   you know!
Proud completion of achievement!" And we paced it, praising still
That soft tread on velvet verdure as it wound through hill and hill;
And at very end there met us, coming from Collonge, the pair
—All our people of the Chalet—two, enough and none to spare.
So, we made for home together, and we reached it as the stars
One by one came lamping—chiefly that prepotency of Mars—
And your last word was "I owe you this enjoyment!"—met with
   "Nay:
With yourself it rests to have a month of morrows like today!"
Then the meal, with talk and laughter, and the news of that rare
   nook
Yet untroubled by the tourist, touched on by no travel-book,

All the same—though latent—patent, hybrid birth of land and sea,
And (our travelled friend assured you)—if such miracle might be—
Comparable for completeness of both blessings—all around
Nature, and, inside her circle, safety from world's sight and
    sound—
Comparable to our Saisiaz. "Hold it fast and guard it well!
Go and see and vouch for certain, then come back and never tell
Living soul but us; and haply, prove our sky from cloud as clear,
There may we four meet, praise fortune just as now, another year!"

Thus you charged him on departure: not without the final charge
"Mind tomorrow's early meeting! We must leave our journey
    marge
Ample for the wayside wonders: there's the stoppage at the inn
Three-parts up the mountain, where the hardships of the track
    begin;
There's the convent worth a visit; but, the triumph crowning all—
There's Salève's own platform facing glory which strikes greatness
    small,
—Blanc, supreme above his earth-brood, needles red and white and
    green,
Horns of silver, fangs of crystal set on edge in his demesne.
So, some three weeks since, we saw them: so, tomorrow we intend
You shall see them likewise; therefore Good Night till tomorrow,
    friend!"
Last, the nothings that extinguish embers of a vivid day:
"What might be the Marshal's next move, what Gambetta's
    counter-play?"
Till the landing on the staircase saw escape the latest spark:
"Sleep you well!" "Sleep but as well, you!"—lazy love quenched,
    all was dark.

Nothing dark next day at sundawn! Up I rose and forth I fared:
Took my plunge within the bath-pool, pacified the watch-dog
    scared,

Saw proceed the transmutation—Jura's black to one gold glow,
Trod your level path that let me drink the morning deep and slow,
Reached the little quarry—ravage recompensed by shrub and fern—
Till the overflowing ardours told me time was for return.
So, return I did, and gaily. But, for once, from no far mound
Waved salute a tall white figure. "Has her sleep been so profound?
Foresight, rather, prudent saving strength for day's expenditure!
Ay, the chamber-window's open: out and on the terrace, sure!"

No, the terrace showed no figure, tall, white, leaning through the
    wreaths,
Tangle-twine of leaf and bloom that intercept the air one breathes,
Interpose between one's love and Nature's loving, hill and dale
Down to where the blue lake's wrinkle marks the river's inrush pale
—Mazy Arve: whereon no vessel but goes sliding white and plain,
Not a steamboat pants from harbour but one hears pulsate amain,
Past the city's congregated peace of homes and pomp of spires
—Man's mild protest that there's something more than Nature, man
    requires,
And that, useful as is Nature to attract the tourist's foot,
Quiet slow sure money-making proves the matter's very root,—
Need for body,—while the spirit also needs a comfort reached
By no help of lake or mountain, but the texts whence Calvin
    preached.
"Here's the veil withdrawn from landscape: up to Jura and beyond,
All awaits us ranged and ready; yet she violates the bond,
Neither leans nor looks nor listens: why is this?" A turn of eye
Took the whole sole answer, gave the undisputed reason "why"!

This dread way you had your summons! No premonitory touch,
As you talked and laughed ('tis told me) scarce a minute ere the
    clutch
Captured you in cold forever. Cold? nay, warm you were as life
When I raised you, while the others used, in passionate poor strife,
All the means that seemed to promise any aid, and all in vain.

Gone you were, and I shall never see that earnest face again

Grow transparent, grow transfigured with the sudden light that leapt,

At the first word's provocation, from the heart-deeps where it slept.

Therefore, paying piteous duty, what seemed You have we consigned

Peacefully to—what I think were, of all earth-beds, to your mind

Most the choice for quiet, yonder: low walls stop the vines' approach,

Lovingly Salève protects you; village-sports will ne'er encroach

On the stranger lady's silence, whom friends bore so kind and well

Thither "just for love's sake,"—such their own word was: and who can tell?

You supposed that few or none had known and loved you in the world:

May be! flower that's full-blown tempts the butterfly, not flower that's furled.

But more learned sense unlocked you, loosed the sheath and let expand

Bud to bell and outspread flower-shape at the least warm touch of hand

—Maybe, throb of heart, beneath which,—quickening farther than it knew,—

Treasure oft was disembosomed, scent all strange and unguessed hue.

Disembosomed, re-embosomed,—must one memory suffice,

Prove I knew an Alpine-rose which all beside named Edelweiss?

Rare thing, red or white, you rest now: two days slumbered through; and since

One day more will see me rid of this same scene whereat I wince,

Tetchy at all sights and sounds and pettish at each idle charm

Proffered me who pace now singly where we two went arm in
  arm,—
I have turned upon my weakness: asked "And what, forsooth,
  prevents
That, this latest day allowed me, I fulfil of her intents
One she had the most at heart—that we should thus again survey
From Salève Mont Blanc together?" Therefore,—dared and done
  today
Climbing,—here I stand: but you—where?

                    If a spirit of the place
Broke the silence, bade me question, promised answer,—what
  disgrace
Did I stipulate "Provided answer suit my hopes, not fears!"
Would I shrink to learn my life-time's limit—days, weeks, months
  or years?
Would I shirk assurance on each point whereat I can but guess—
"Does the soul survive the body? Is there God's self, no or yes?"
If I know my mood, 'twere constant—come in whatsoe'er uncouth
Shape it should, nay, formidable—so the answer were but truth.

Well, and wherefore shall it daunt me, when 'tis I myself am
  tasked,
When, by weakness weakness questioned, weakly answers—weakly
  asked?
Weakness never needs be falseness: truth is truth in each degree
—Thunderpealed by God to Nature, whispered by my soul to me.
Nay, the weakness turns to strength and triumphs in a truth
  beyond:
"Mine is but man's truest answer—how were it did God respond?"
I shall no more dare to mimic such response in futile speech,
Pass off human lisp as echo of the sphere-song out of reach,
Than,—because it well may happen yonder, where the far snows
  blanch

Mute Mont Blanc, that who stands near them sees and hears an
   avalanche,—
I shall pick a clod and throw,—cry "Such the sight and such the
   sound!
What though I nor see nor hear them? Others do, the proofs
   abound!"
Can I make my eye an eagle's, sharpen ear to recognize
Sound o'er league and league of silence? Can I know, who but
   surmise?
If I dared no self-deception when, a week since, I and you
Walked and talked along the grass-path, passing lightly in review
What seemed hits and what seemed misses in a certain
   fence-play,—strife
Sundry minds of mark engaged in "On the Soul and Future
   Life,"—
If I ventured estimating what was come of parried thrust,
Subtle stroke, and, rightly, wrongly, estimating could be just
—Just, though life so seemed abundant in the form which moved
   by mine,
I might well have played at feigning, fooling,—laughed "What
   need opine
Pleasure must succeed to pleasure, else past pleasure turns to pain,
And this first life claims a second, else I count its good no gain?"—
Much less have I heart to palter when the matter to decide
Now becomes "Was ending ending once and always, when you
   died?"
Did the face, the form I lifted as it lay, reveal the loss
Not alone of life but soul? A tribute to yon flowers and moss,
What of you remains beside? A memory! Easy to attest
"Certainly from out the world that one believes who knew her best
Such was good in her, such fair, which fair and good were great
   perchance
Had but fortune favoured, bidden each shy faculty advance;
After all—who knows another? Only as I know, I speak."

So much of you lives within me while I live my year or week.
Then my fellow takes the tale up, not unwilling to aver
Duly in his turn "I knew him best of all, as he knew her:
Such he was, and such he was not, and such other might have been
But that somehow every actor, somewhere in this earthly scene,
Fails." And so both memories dwindle, yours and mine together
        linked,
Till there is but left for comfort, when the last spark proves
        extinct,
This—that somewhere new existence led by men and women new
Possibly attains perfection coveted by me and you;
While ourselves, the only witness to what work our life evolved,
Only to ourselves proposing problems proper to be solved
By ourselves alone,—who working ne'er shall know if work bear
        fruit
Others reap and garner, heedless how produced by stalk and root,—
We who, darkling, timed the day's birth,—struggling, testified to
        peace,—
Earned, by dint of failure, triumph,—we, creative thought, must
        cease
In created word, thought's echo, due to impulse long since sped!
Why repine? There's ever someone lives although ourselves be
        dead!

Well, what signifies repugnance? Truth is truth howe'er it strike.
Fair or foul the lot apportioned life on earth, we bear alike.
Stalwart body idly yoked to stunted spirit, powers, that fain
Else would soar, condemned to grovel, groundlings through the
        fleshly chain,—
Help that hinders, hindrance proved but help disguised when all too
        late,—
Hindrance is the fact acknowledged, howsoe'er explained as Fate,
Fortune, Providence: we bear, own life a burthen more or less.
Life thus owned unhappy, is there supplemental happiness

Possible and probable in life to come? or must we count
Life a curse and not a blessing, summed-up in its whole amount,
Help and hindrance, joy and sorrow?

                      Why should I want courage here?
I will ask and have an answer,—with no favour, with no fear,—
From myself. How much, how little, do I inwardly believe
True that controverted doctrine? Is it fact to which I cleave,
Is it fancy I but cherish, when I take upon my lips
Phrase the solemn Tuscan fashioned, and declare the soul's eclipse
Not the soul's extinction? take his "I believe and I declare—
Certain am I—from this life I pass into a better, there
Where that lady lives of whom enamoured was my soul"—where
    this
Other lady, my companion dear and true, she also is?

I have questioned and am answered. Question, answer presuppose
Two points: that the thing itself which questions, answers,—*is,* it
    knows;
As it also knows the thing perceived outside itself,—a force
Actual ere its own beginning, operative through its course,
Unaffected by its end,—that this thing likewise needs must be;
Call this—God, then, call that—soul, and both—the only facts for
    me.
Prove them facts? that they o'erpass my power of proving, proves
    them such:
Fact it is I know I know not something which is fact as much.
What before caused all the causes, what effect of all effects
Haply follows,—these are fancy. Ask the rush if it suspects
Whence and how the stream which floats it had a rise, and where
    and how
Falls or flows on still! What answer makes the rush except that
    now
Certainly it floats and is, and, no less certain than itself,
Is the everyway external stream that now through shoal and shelf

Floats it onward, leaves it—may be—wrecked at last, or lands on
    shore
There to root again and grow and flourish stable evermore.
—May be! mere surmise not knowledge: much conjecture styled
    belief,
What the rush conceives the stream means through the voyage
    blind and brief.
Why, because I doubtless am, shall I as doubtless be? "Because
God seems good and wise." Yet under this our life's apparent laws
Reigns a wrong which, righted once, would give quite other laws
    to life.
"He seems potent." Potent here, then: why are right and wrong at
    strife?

FROM *DRAMATIC IDYLS: SECOND SERIES,* 1880

Pan and Luna

Si credere dignum est.
Georgic. iii. 390.

O worthy of belief I hold it was,
Virgil, your legend in those strange three lines!
No question, that adventure came to pass
One black night in Arcadia: yes, the pines,
Mountains and valleys mingling made one mass
Of black with void black heaven: the earth's confines,
The sky's embrace,—below, above, around,
All hardened into black without a bound.

Fill up a swart stone chalice to the brim
With fresh-squeezed yet fast-thickening poppy-juice:
See how the sluggish jelly, late a-swim,
Turns marble to the touch of who would loose

The solid smooth, grown jet from rim to rim,
By turning round the bowl! So night can fuse
Earth with her all-comprising sky. No less,
Light, the least spark, shows air and emptiness.

And thus it proved when—diving into space,
Stript of all vapour, from each web of mist
Utterly film-free—entered on her race
The naked Moon, full-orbed antagonist
Of night and dark, night's dowry: peak to base,
Upstarted mountains, and each valley, kissed
To sudden life, lay silver-bright: in air
Flew she revealed, Maid-Moon with limbs all bare.

Still as she fled, each depth—where refuge seemed—
Opening a lone pale chamber, left distinct
Those limbs: 'mid still-retreating blue, she teemed
Herself with whiteness,—virginal, uncinct
By any halo save what finely gleamed
To outline not disguise her: heaven was linked
In one accord with earth to quaff the joy,
Drain beauty to the dregs without alloy.

Whereof she grew aware. What help? When, lo,
A succourable cloud with sleep lay dense:
Some pine-tree top had caught it sailing slow,
And tethered for a prize: in evidence
Captive lay fleece on fleece of piled-up snow
Drowsily patient: flake-heaped how or whence,
The structure of that succourable cloud,
What matter? Shamed she plunged into its shroud.

Orbed—so the woman-figure poets call
Because of rounds on rounds—that apple-shaped
Head which its hair binds close into a ball

Each side the curving ears—that pure undraped
Pout of the sister paps—that . . . Once for all,
Say—her consummate circle thus escaped
With its innumerous circlets, sank absorbed,
Safe in the cloud—O naked Moon full-orbed!

But what means this? The downy swathes combine,
Conglobe, the smothery coy-caressing stuff
Curdles about her! Vain each twist and twine
Those lithe limbs try, encroached on by a fluff
Fitting as close as fits the dented spine
Its flexile ivory outside-flesh: enough!
The plumy drifts contract, condense, constringe,
Till she is swallowed by the feathery springe.

As when a pearl slips lost in the thin foam
Churned on a sea-shore, and, o'er-frothed, conceits
Herself safe-housed in Amphitrite's dome,—
If, through the bladdery wave-worked yeast, she meets
What most she loathes and leaps from,—elf from gnome
No gladlier,—finds that safest of retreats
Bubble about a treacherous hand wide ope
To grasp her—(divers who pick pearls so grope)—

So lay this Maid-Moon clasped around and caught
By rough red Pan, the god of all that tract:
He it was schemed the snare thus subtly wrought
With simulated earth-breath,—wool-tufts packed
Into a billowy wrappage. Sheep far-sought
For spotless shearings yield such: take the fact
As learned Virgil gives it,—how the breed
Whitens itself for ever: yes, indeed!

If one forefather ram, though pure as chalk
From tinge on fleece, should still display a tongue

Black 'neath the beast's moist palate, prompt men balk
The propagating plague: he gets no young:
They rather slay him,—sell his hide to caulk
Ships with, first steeped in pitch,—nor hands are wrung
In sorrow for his fate: protected thus,
The purity we love is gained for us.

So did Girl-moon, by just her attribute
Of unmatched modesty betrayed, lie trapped,
Bruised to the breast of Pan, half-god half-brute,
Raked by his bristly boar-sward while he lapped
—Never say, kissed her! that were to pollute
Love's language—which moreover proves unapt
To tell how she recoiled—as who finds thorns
Where she sought flowers—when, feeling, she touched—horns!

Then—does the legend say?—first moon-eclipse
Happened, first swooning-fit which puzzled sore
The early sages? Is that why she dips
Into the dark, a minute and no more,
Only so long as serves her while she rips
The cloud's womb through and, faultless as before,
Pursues her way? No lesson for a maid
Left she, a maid herself thus trapped, betrayed?

Ha, Virgil? Tell the rest, you! "To the deep
Of his domain the wildwood, Pan forthwith
Called her, and so she followed"—in her sleep,
Surely?—"by no means spurning him." The myth
Explain who may! Let all else go, I keep
—As of a ruin just a monolith—
Thus much, one verse of five words, each a boon:
Arcadia, night, a cloud, Pan, and the moon.

About the Editor

❖❖

Douglas Dunn was born in Scotland in 1942 and grew up there in the village of Inchinnan. He worked in libraries for several years before attending the University of Hull, from which he graduated in 1969. In 1971 he resigned from the library of the university to become a free-lance writer. Faber and Faber published his eight books of verse, the most recent being Elegies *(1985),* Selected Poems *(1986), and* Northlight *(1988). The Ecco Press published* New and Selected Poems *in 1989. He has received the Somerset Maugham Award, the Geoffrey Faber Memorial Prize, the Hawthornden Prize, and the Whitbread Prize for Poetry.* Elegies *was chosen as the Whitbread Book of the Year for 1985. Dunn has also published a collection of short stories,* Secret Villages *(Faber and Faber, and Dodd, Mead, 1985) and occasionally contributes fiction to* The New Yorker *and other publications. He has written plays for BBC radio and television. Dunn is an honorary professor of the University of Dundee, an honorary fellow of Humberside College, a fellow of the Royal Society of Literature, and an honorary doctor of laws of the University of Dundee. He lives in Fife, Scotland, and is currently writer-in-residence at the University of St. Andrews.*